CONTENTS

■ ■ ■

PREFACE

■ ■ ■

This little book arose out of my experience of teaching European history for sixteen years—first at Gettysburg College and then at my alma mater, the University of Tennessee, Knoxville—and then out of the sixteen years I spent directing the Expository Writing Program at Harvard, where I regularly taught a course called "Writing about History."

Most students came into my courses believing that history was hardly more than a collection of names and dates to be memorized and repeated on examinations. They thought they could go to the library, look up several articles in encyclopedias, and write a paper to show how much they knew about a subject. They did not imagine that they could think for themselves about the facts. Sometimes they believed that "thinking" was to express vehement opinions, often about the supposed morality or immorality of the past they read and wrote about. Far too often they tried to write as though they were accomplished historians who had solved all the problems about some broad historical subject and could only scorn those who disagreed with them.

It was my job to teach them that history becomes most exciting when we study a collection of primary sources—the basic stuff from which history is made—to make sense of these sources and tell a story about them. Primary sources are by definition the sources closest to the events and people whose stories we seek to tell. They may be letters, diaries, and books published by participants in events. Woodrow Wilson, Thomas More, Martin Luther King, Jr., Virginia Woolf, Eleanor Roosevelt, and Toni Morrison all wrote extensively or spoke so that their words were recorded by others. These written materials are primary sources for their lives. Or primary sources may be the earliest reports of those who knew or claimed to know figures in the past whom we study in the present.

Historians and others have written about these primary sources. They have produced secondary sources—narratives, interpretations, and descriptions—to tell us what they think the primary sources mean. These secondary sources, as we call them, embody hard work and careful thought—and often disagree with one another. No one serious about the study of history can neglect this treasury of research and thought, and students should demonstrate in the papers they write in college that they are familiar with what other people have written about a topic. The best history papers show a balance between primary and secondary sources.

The best reasons for studying history are the same as those for studying all the liberal arts: historical study satisfies curiosity, and it enriches our minds. The most interesting human beings are those with curiosity. They ask questions. How did things get to be the way they are? Why have some names come down to us glittering with fame or stained with infamy? Why is this monument here? Why was this painting a scandal when it was first shown to the public? How did this book cause a revolution? Who built this amazing bridge?

History also provides us with the pleasure of vicarious experience—living in our imaginations lives others have lived in the past. It opens windows into the variety of human experience and reveals human nature, not in some abstract philosophical way but in the concrete actuality of what real human beings thought and did. History tells us how diverse human beings and their societies can be. If we study it attentively, it should make us more tolerant of people unlike ourselves because history reveals such an immense variety of successful human experiences.

The study of history has expanded in recent years. Only a generation or two ago in the United States, historians thought that the only history worth attention consisted of war and politics and that the only historical figures worth studying were great men, especially great men in Western Europe and the United States. Now historians study the history of women, the history of minorities in various countries including our own, the history of popular culture, the history of sexual practices, the history of science, military history, and heaven knows what else.

Teaching people to write about history has been for me a means of showing students of all ages that they have worthwhile thoughts and can use them to write interesting and original essays on many subjects. As users of this book will, I hope, discover, the study of history involves a special kind of thinking, closely related to the way we solve puzzles and try to guess who the murderer is in a good mystery. Historical thinking is indeed a kind of game, and it has a deeply serious side—but it is also a lot of fun!

I hope *A Short Guide to Writing about History* will continue to help students think about history, see its puzzles and its pleasures, and gain the confidence that good writing about anything requires. You must approach the task with the trust that you have the tools to do the job, and I hope you will find them in this little book.

RICHARD MARIUS
1998

SOME NOTES ON THE FOURTH EDITION

Since its first edition a dozen years ago, this *Short Guide* has been an essential part of many college students' adventure with writing history papers. I have always found it useful for my students as they have tried coming to grips with methods historians employ in research and writing about the past. More than that, though, the commitment of Professor Marius to such endeavors was unstinting. As he promised, those who wrote to him with questions were not disappointed; and on several different occasions he joined my entire class for organized listserv discussions of historical research and writing. His insights were always helpful and to-the-point for my students. And they certainly were important to me as I attempted to teach the excitement of historical study.

There is no question of the importance that Richard Marius had in shaping a new generation of historians. Following his untimely death in late 1999, editors at Longman were determined to keep his advice available for still more students in the twenty-first century. I am honored that they asked me to prepare this edition of *A Short Guide to Writing About History* and grateful for the conversations I previously had with Richard about this book which have helped me immeasurably in doing so. While I have tried to ensure this fourth edition reflects the widespread agreement we had about the craft of historical writing, it naturally echoes a number of my own concerns as well. By seeking to join our thoughts on these matters, however, I believe this fourth edition is a stronger *Guide* for students.

Readers familiar with the third edition will notice the greatest changes in attempts to take cognizance of the evolving realm of electronic resources for historians. This continues an effort begun in the third edition. I have tried to treat these ongoing changes in the profession both more broadly and more generally at the same time. This edition contains two new Chapters, 4 and 5, each of which extend the previous discussions of Gathering Information, Taking Notes, and Writing Drafts more fully into the electronic environment. For example, there is greater emphasis on general principles of dealing with electronic sources and communications rather than on a very specific advice. I encourage students to apply (and thus practice) essential historical skills of evidence evaluation as they locate materials on the World Wide Web. Thus, there are no lists of "excellent history websites," for example, although I have included a few suggestions for using particularly valuable Internet materials which show promise of long-term accessibility.

The fourth edition also contains some suggestions about note taking, writing, and revising in an electronic environment. Again, I have emphasized basic principals rather than providing step-by-step instructions of how to operate a word processing program (for example). I have assumed that students (and their instructors) have some understanding of popular and widely used computer programs and, with just a little guidance, are capable of learning more about specific operations—and about new programs—on their own. With Professor Marius, I have great faith in both the intelligence and tenacity—as well as the curiosity—of our student readers. And I also believe that detailed instructions and specific advice about the use of word-processing and management programs can best be taught and learned when working on specific projects with specific programs; the great variety of both also mitigated the specific advice which I might offer in a *Short Guide*.

Similar emphasis on electronic resources for writing have been included in the substantially revised Chapters 7 and 8, with suggestions about both writing Conventions and Documenting Sources using word-processing techniques. For example, I have offered advice about how to make citations to materials uncovered using the search utilities found on many historically oriented web sites. And I encourage students to avoid using *ibid.* in their note citations, as doing so may sometimes lead to confusions when trying to move text from one section of their papers to another using the common block, cut, and paste methods which are otherwise very helpful to writers working with a word-processing program.

I have also tried to continue the tenor of previous revisions in this fourth edition. There are more examples drawn from writing about world history, including a student essay (here presented as Appendix A) which views an idea in American history from a global perspective. And Appendix B, concerning book reviews, has been expanded to include a student review and a review of the same book from a historical journal. In keeping with the inclusion of more women historians in the third edition, the samples of student work included in the fourth edition were written by two of my female students. Finally, I have throughout consolidated and extended the "Writer's Checklist" approach. While none of these condensed guides to better writing are intended to be viewed as "rules," per se, the checklists should offer concise guidance for writers seeking a quick review of essential elements of our advice on the research and writing process.

I am eager to hear from readers about experiences with this book. Please write to me with any thoughts you have about *A Short Guide to Writing about History*. Letters may be sent by post to me at the History Department, East Tennessee State University, Johnson City, TN 34614. You may also write using my e-mail address, <pagem@etsu.edu>. As did Professor Marius, I shall always respond.

ACKNOWLEDGMENTS

A number of historians at various colleges and universities offered priceless advice in the preparation of the manuscript for various editions of *A Short Guide to Writing about History*. I am particularly grateful to those whose thoughtful comments helped shape this fourth edition:

Benjamin D. Berry, Jr., Virginia Wesleyan College

Jeff Charles, California State University, San Marcos

Risa Faussette, College of Saint Rose

Michael G. Galgano, James Madison University

Beverly Garrison, Oral Roberts University

Randolph Hollingsworth, Kentucky Virtual University

Pamela Hronek, Arkansas State University

T. Mills Kelly, Texas Tech University

Lezlie S. Knox, California State University, Long Beach

Cynthia J. Kosso, Northern Arizona University

Kenneth. J. Orosz, University of Maine at Farmington

Linda A. Pollock, Tulane University of Louisiana

James E. Sherow, Kansas State University

Daniel Thorp, Virginia Tech

I also appreciate the support I have had from colleagues at three universities where I have taught about historical writing and research:

Murray State University, the University of Natal-Durban (South Africa), and East Tennessee State University. While all my colleagues have influenced my thinking about these subjects in one way or another, I especially appreciate conversations with Ken Wolf, Jim Odom, and Doug Burgess on many details concerning historical research and writing. In addition, Henry Antkiewicz, Ronnie Day, Steve Fritz, Allan Rushing, and Dale Schmitt at ETSU have provided particular suggestions which I believe have improved the work. I have learned much, as well, from my students who shared with me their frustrations and triumphs in historical research and writing; Michael Banner, Sabrina Shilad, and Penny Sonnenburg have made specific contributions to this volume. And at Addison Wesley Longman I appreciate the confidence of Susan Westmoreland and the consistent advice and ongoing encouragement of Susan Kunchandy who literally made this book happen.

Most of all, this would not be possible without the road laid down by Richard Marius years ago. Collaborators such as him are hard to find. I count myself fortunate, indeed.

MELVIN E. PAGE

INTRODUCTION

■ ■ ■

Students struggling over an essay in history have often told us that they know the subject, but they cannot write about it. They usually mean that they have a jumble of facts in their heads but cannot tell a story about them.

Their complaint represents a discovery: History *does* involve telling a story, and while facts are essential in telling a story, they are not enough. You can have a big, bad wolf, a little girl named Red Riding Hood, an old grandmother, a basket of cakes, and a dark wood without having a story. You can even know the date of the wolf's birth, the color of Red Riding Hood's hair, and the mailing address of the grandmother as well as her Social Security number, and still not have a story. Stories have tension, usually presented right at the beginning. At the start we know that something will happen. People and forces contend with each other. Readers see tension, struggle, and the possibility that something is out of balance, and they read on to see how it all comes out.

STORIES ABOUT THE PAST INTENDED TO BE TRUE

In writing an essay about history, you tell the story of your thinking about a topic wherein forces are opposed to each other with the outcome in doubt. You formulate a thesis to say that things happened this way and not another and that the reason they happened this way was because of this, this, and this! You allow for the possibility that if this or this, or that, did not happen, things could have turned out entirely differently.

Historians study sources that tell them about the past, and they write because they see something that needs to be explained. Like journalists, they ask who, what, where, when, and why. Who was responsible? What happened? Where did this event happen? When or in what order did things happen? Why did they happen? What have other historians said about the event? What mistakes did they make that I can now correct? The historian is a curious and relentless questioner.

Historians are like most of the rest of us. They want to know what events mean, why they were important to what came afterwards, why we still talk about them. When the people of Israel crossed the Jordan River into Palestine, or "Canaan" after their Exodus from Egypt and their wandering in the desert, their leader Joshua commanded them to take twelve heavy stones from the river and set them in a pile on the western bank. He said that in years to come when children asked their parents, "What do you mean by these stones?" the parents would tell the story of how Israel crossed the Jordan with God's help. The stones were a memorial; that is, they made generations of Israelites remember. They made children ask questions that adults could answer.

Our public monuments do the same. A child standing below the Capitol of the United States—the great sculptured likeness of Ulysses S. Grant astride his horse, looking south across the Washington Mall under the brim of his hat—will ask his or her parents, "Who is that?" And the parents can say, "This is the man who saved the Union, and made us a nation."

Questions rise from our monuments, our habits, our documents, our broader experience in the world. All historical writing begins as an effort to answer questions about origins, happenings, and consequences. We find a puzzle and try to solve it. When you write a paper for a history course, you must do the same—find a problem that stirs your curiosity and try to solve it. If you don't have a problem, you don't have a paper. Here are the first two paragraphs of an article in *The American Historical Review* (*AHR*), the leading journal for historians in the United States:

In France during the 1920s, fashion was a highly charged issue. In 1925, an article in a journal called *L'oeuvre* ["The Work"] described how the fashion of short hair had completely overturned life in a small French village. After the first woman in the village cut her hair, accompanied by "tears and grinding of teeth" on the part of her family, the fashion had quickly become "epidemic: from house to house, it took its victims." A gardener swore he would lock up his daughter until her hair grew back; a husband believed that his wife had dishonored him. A scandalized priest decided to preach a sermon about it, but "unfortunately he had chosen the wrong day, since it was the feast of Jeanne d'Arc." As he began to condemn bobbed hair as indecent and unchristian, "the most impudent young ladies of the parish pointed insolently at the statue of the liberator." By claiming the bobbed-cut Joan of Arc as their mascot, these young women grounded their quest for "liberation" in the rich, tangled mainstream of French history. They appealed to the ambivalent yet strongly traditional image of *Jeanne la pucelle* (Joan the Virgin), at once patriotic, fervently Christian, and sexually ambiguous.

The fashion among young women for short, bobbed hair created enormous tensions within the French family. Throughout the decade, newspapers recorded lurid tales, including one husband in the provinces who sequestered his wife for bobbing her hair and another father who reportedly killed his daughter for the same reason. A father in Dijon sought legal action against a hairdresser in 1925 for cuffing the hair of his daughter without his authority. "At present, the question of short hair is dividing families," argued Antoine, one of the hairdressers who pioneered the bobbed cut. "The result," according to journalist Paul Reboux, "was that during family meals, nothing is heard except the clicking of the forks on the porcelain." One working-class woman, who was in her twenties during the era, remembered that her mother-in-law did not talk to her sister-in-law Simone for almost a year after the latter bobbed her hair. René Rambaud, another hairdresser who helped to popularize the cut, recalled the story of a newly married woman who cut her hair, believing that she had the right to do so without consulting her parents. Her mother and father in turn accused her husband and his parents of the monstrous crime, leading to a rift so severe that the two families did not reconcile for twenty years.'[1]

We read these few anecdotes and ask ourselves, "What was all the fuss about?" We expect answers, and Professor Mary Louise Roberts gives them to us. In her last past paragraph she sums up her conclusions:

> For historians trying to understand socio-cultural changes during the period of World War I, the controversy surrounding postwar fashion is a rich source for exploration. The ways in which French observers read the text of fashion can tell us much about what preoccupied and worried them during this time of transition. Many of the French, such as fashion's critics, yearned for a more traditional and stable French society, symbolized by the domestic hearth. They expressed anxiety that change would usher in a colder, more impersonal world. Others, namely the supporters of fashion, welcomed change as a dismissal of pre-war social constraints. Fashion was not "politics" as we are used to conceiving of it, but the debates over its meaning in postwar France were profoundly political. The fashions of the modern woman became central to the cultural mythology of the era, instilling at once envy, admiration, frustration, and horror, because they provided both a visual language for upheaval and changed and figured in a political struggle for the redefinition of female identity.[2]

Professor Roberts, stirred by curiosity, sought the answer to a question: Why did the French after World War I make so much of the decision of some French women to cut their hair short? Today we may find it puzzling that anyone could care how women cut their hair. That puzzle interested Professor Roberts, and she wrote an essay to solve it.

---

[1] Mary Louise Roberts, "Samson and Delilah Revisited: The Politics of Women's Fashion in 1920s France," *The American Historical Review* 98 (1993): 657–658. We have left out Professor Roberts's extensive footnotes for these paragraphs.

[2] Roberts, "Samson and Delilah Revisited," 684.

Solving the puzzles of history involves science and art. Science is a synonym for knowledge. But knowledge of what? History includes data—evidence, the names of people and places, when things happened, where they happened, bits of information gathered from many sources. It also includes interpretations of historians and others in the past who have written on the topic that the writer decides to treat in an essay. The art of history lies in combining fact and interpretation to tell a story about the past. Professor Roberts did that in her article. She had data—the reports of the controversy stirred up in France when women cut their hair short after World War I. Her essay interprets what the data mean.

As time passes, legends and outright lies also creep into history. Historians try to distinguish between the true and the false. Thus their stories, as the late Professor J. H. Hexter was fond of saying, are a "patterned, coherent account of the human past intended to be true,"[3] as distinguished from the fiction of novels and short stories, for example. In the sixteenth century some English writers called history "authentic stories" to distinguish it from fantastic tales about the past. Historians in the Renaissance set about examining sources, making judgments about what could be believed and what not. They searched for old documents, studied them to see if they were authentic, weeded out forgeries, and compared copies to find errors scribes had made in transmitting texts. They also compared different stories told about the same events. These historians tried to tell the truth—just as do historians today.

But in the study of history, "truth" is complicated, contradictory, and usually obscure. History does not repeat itself. Every historical event happens one time and becomes separated from the present by the steady accumulation of other events happening day by day. We cannot put the assassination of President John F. Kennedy into a laboratory and make it happen again and again as we might conduct an experiment in chemistry, measuring and calculating to

---

[3] J. H. Hexter, *The History Primer* (New York: Basic Books, 1971), 5.

see precisely the relations of cause and effect. The event happened once—on Friday, November 22, 1963—and it will never happen again. To know that event we depend on the memories of those who were there, and, as they die off, the records they left us of Kennedy's death. These records may include sound and video recordings that make his murder more vivid than books and articles can. But they are all records, subject to many interpretations and subject also to the tricks memory plays even on eyewitnesses. We can never relive the event exactly as it happened.

All historians confront an essential problem: The past is dissolving under our feet at every moment. The Romans had a proverb: *Tempus edax rerum*, "Time is the devourer of things." Time destroys. The evidence for past events is always incomplete and fragmentary; many pieces of evidence are lost, and others are often faded and warped. Historians fit the pieces together as carefully as possible, but holes remain in the picture they try to reconstruct. They do their best to fill in the holes with inferences that seem plausible and that fit the available facts. What emerges may closely resemble what happened, but we can never be sure that what we know as history is exactly right. Our knowledge of history is always in flux, and historians are always in dialogue, not only with the primary sources of the events they write about but also with other historians of those events. To write history is to be engaged in endless argument.

WRITING HISTORY AS A WAY OF THINKING

History and writing are inseparable. We cannot know history well unless we write about it. Writing allows us to arrange events and our thoughts, study our work, weed out contradictions, get names and places right, and question interpretations—our own and those of other historians. In writing we work out the chronological order of events—not a simple task but one indispensable to the historian's craft.

Fluent talkers can touch on first one idea and then another, sometimes using body language to stress a point. They can overwhelm opposition by charisma or by shouting when their argument is weak. Writers perform a more daring act! They must develop an idea with logic and clarity, knowing that a reader can study their words again and again and discover whether the words add up to a plausible argument, given the evidence available. If writers are illogical, unfair, untruthful, confused, or foolish, their words lie on the page to be attacked by anyone with the care and interest to look. Good talkers can contradict themselves, waffle, and weasel, and, on being called to task, can claim that their hearers misunderstood them, or they can say, "I didn't say that at all." Because our short-term memory is fallible, we may think we have indeed misunderstood. Because we are also usually polite, we may allow sloppy talkers to escape their confused expression by their dexterity in shifting words. Writers enjoy no such emergency exit. What they have written they have written, and it is on the page for all to see again and again. Writers must strive to be clear, logical, and fair, or they will be found out.

Good writing goes hand in hand with a sense of human possibility and limitation. No wonder that in some societies, such as ancient Israel, historians were priestly figures. They wrote in the light of their beliefs about the relation of God to humankind and therefore with an idea of human nature and the purpose of life. Our beliefs about what is possible for human beings will control our beliefs about what might have happened in the past. Can men and women be heroic? Are human beings always selfish, or can we be truly generous? Does human history move in response to leaders or in spite of them? Or are leaders thrust up by the society that in fact leads them? Are our strongest motivations for power, for wealth, for sex, or for community? Are we naturally aggressive, or do we prefer peace?

As important as any other question about human nature is this: Do we have any freedom of choice? Is history a series of important decisions that could have gone either way? Or is it a masquerade, a perpetual series of predestined events that no human will can control? Did Robert E. Lee have to fight the battle of Gettysburg as he did, or did he have a choice? Did President Harry S. Truman have a choice when he decided to drop the atom bombs on Japan to end World War II in 1945? Was the bomb necessary to end the war and to prevent an invasion of Japan in which millions of lives would have been lost? Or was he driven by the desire for revenge against Japan and the wish to make a demonstration of power against the Soviet Union after Japan was already effectively beaten? Or are all these explanations at least partly true?

Historians usually write as if people had the power to choose in the past. The tension between what historical figures did and what they might have done gives history part of its excitement. Herbert Butterfield, a philosopher of history, wrote, "History deals with the drama of human life as the affair of individual personalities, possessing self-consciousness, intellect, and freedom."[4] Tolstoy, by contrast, in his novel *War and Peace* wrestled with the idea of freedom, observing that "to conceive a man perfectly free, not subject to the law of necessity, we must conceive of a man *outside of space, outside of time, and free from all dependence on cause.*"[5] He wrestled with the problem of just how much freedom we have and what part of life is constrained by necessity. He concluded that leaders only *seem* to lead—that in fact they emerge out of the collective development of a power inherent in the masses of people. In writing about the past, historians may not say explicitly that their answers depend on their view of human nature or human freedom. Yet their answers depend on assumptions, sometimes unexpressed, about what is possible or probable in human nature and what is not.

Every part of the past has a unique quality. Every event we study in history existed in its own network of cause and effect, its

---

[4] Herbert Butterfleld, *Christianity and History* (New York: Scribner's, 1950), 26.

[5] Leo Tolstoy, *War and Peace*, trans. Constance Garnett (New York: Modern Library, n.d.), 1131.

own set of relations between people and events, its own modes of thought, usually taken for granted by the societies themselves, often assumed to be a divine ordination that could not be changed. A thunderstorm roars over the Kansas prairie today, and the unflappable television news meteorologist explains that the storm is the result of a collision between a cold front and a warm front. In ancient Mesopotamia, the Babylonians heard in the thunder the voice of their god Marduk and thought that he was hurling lightning bolts into the earth. In these and countless other ways, spontaneous responses to many experiences in the past were different from our own. Part of our task is to think our way into the minds of the people who lived in earlier times so we can think about experience as they did.

Yet we can never fully abandon our own perceptions; we cannot recover the past exactly as people then thought of life and the world. Historians must always put something of themselves into the stories they tell; never are they empty vessels through which the records of the past are transformed into untouched truths about a past. This inevitable insertion of the historian into historical accounts is what J. H. Hexter called an application of "the second record," encompassing "everything which historians bring to their confrontation with the record of the past."[6] While this is an inevitable legacy of the historian's work, it is one we must always seek to keep it in check lest the stories which emerge lose any semblance of credulity. And that is a crucial test: are the stories, as well as the explanations and analysis they offer, credible?

Sometimes historians try to distinguish between the unique qualities in events and the qualities that seem to repeat themselves. What qualities help some large states endure? What qualities doom others to fall? The earliest great empires in Western civilization were made possible when people learned to ride horses shortly after 2000 B.C. Armies on horseback could pass swiftly from place to place, appearing suddenly, striking terror in soldiers inexperienced with the noise and

---

[6] Hexter, *History Primer*, 79.

speed of such mighty animals. These empires rose swiftly and then swiftly collapsed. But centuries afterward the Roman Empire rose and endured for centuries. What circumstances made these early empires rise and fall with such bewildering speed? How was Rome different? Would our study of Assyria and Babylon illuminate in any way our understanding of the sudden and unexpected collapse of the Soviet Union? The questions are fascinating, but the answers are uncertain. One historian may see a pattern of repetition; another may see, in the same events, circumstances unique to a specific time and place.

Some Greek and Roman historians believed that history involved cycles of repetition and that to know the past allowed them to predict the future. Few modern historians would make such claims. Some broad patterns repeat themselves. Empires, countries, and cultures rise and fall. Protests against a dominant culture often show up in how people—especially young people—dress and wear their hair. To some scholars, these repetitions make it seem that all history is locked into invariable cycles. History becomes a treadmill on which human beings toil endlessly without getting anywhere.

Many nineteenth-century historians believed that history was the story of inevitable progress, culminating in the triumph of the white races because of their supposed superiority over people of color throughout the world. If today is good, tomorrow will be better. Other historians have seen history moving according to God's will. When people do good, they thrive; when they violate the laws of God, they decline and suffer. But on close investigation, the swirls and waves of the historical process don't appear to move in predictable patterns.

Those who assume that learning about the past will allow them to avoid mistakes in the future underestimate the continuous flow of the new into human events. New inventions or new ways of thinking or new combinations can upset all predictions. In 1914 both the French and the German generals in charge of planning for a war between their two countries expected the coming conflict to resemble the war between Germany and France in 1870–1871. In that earlier war, the Germans moved swiftly by railroad and on horseback, outmaneuvered the French, and determined the outcome of the war within three months. It was a war of motion—dramatic, soon over, without much damage to either side in property or human life. In 1914 both sides expected another short war, not recognizing the destructive power of a new weapon, the machine gun, which ultimately created a near daily massacre that turned the conflict into a four-year standoff in opposing lines of trenches running from the Swiss border to the English Channel. In this long, hard war, millions died, and the north of France was devastated.

In 1940 the French, learning from the fatal experience of World War I, built a series of concrete forts across northern France called the Maginot Line, anticipating another war in which armies would face each other until one dropped from exhaustion. The Maginot Line was to be a sort of warm, dry, and safe trench made of reinforced concrete. The French planned without considering the new technology of that era—airplanes and swift armored tanks—which was later used by the Germans to defeat the French in forty days of *Blitzkrieg* (lightning war).

At the very least, experiences such as these teach us to be cautious in suggesting what history can tell us of both present and future. For one thing, we no longer predict inevitable progress in human affairs. We can know history well and still be startled by events. In recent decades, thousands of historians young and old studied the history of the Soviet Union. The Central Intelligence Agency employed historians to help our government understand how to deal with the Soviet Union and predict what it might do. Yet not one of these scholars predicted anything like the sudden collapse and breakup of the great Soviet empire in 1989 and 1990. And certainly none believed that President Reagan's characterization of the Soviet Union as an "evil empire" would precipitate its disintegration.

But what of the place of leaders in history? The current mood in historical studies is to be skeptical about how much individual leaders may accomplish on their own. We seem to be closer to Tolstoy than to Butterfield. Historians know that any particular event in history is brought into being by a complex of contributing forces—some visible and some difficult to identify. What caused the American Revolution? The popular answer was oppression of American colonies by Britain, the mother country, and most of us can probably recite events that goaded the colonies to revolt—the Stamp Act, the Boston Massacre, the tax on tea and the consequent Boston Tea Party, and finally the skirmishes at Lexington and Concord on April 19, 1775, when someone fired "the shot heard 'round the world." Leaders such as John Hancock, Sam Adams, John Adams, James Otis, and others in Massachusetts were said to be leaders of an almost unanimous populace. That, at least, was the history of the American Revolution as many of us learned it in grade school and in the popular mythology spread by Fourth of July oratory.

On examination, British "oppression" seems much less severe than once commonly supposed, American support for the Revolution far less than unanimous, and leadership of the patriot forces much more ambiguous. Historians now search for deeper causes that provoked a substantial number of Americans to want their independence from Great Britain enough to fight for it. Yes, Americans had great orators such as Sam Adams and Patrick Henry. But orators are nothing unless they have an audience, and our experience in the present shows us that orators don't change people's minds so much as they provide words for feelings that people already have. What groups were dissatisfied and willing to listen to the patriot orators? Why? What groups were content under British rule, and why? What role did American women and the American clergy play? To what degree was the American Revolution a class struggle within colonial American society? How much of the Revolution's success came because the British were more concerned with their war with France than with their rebellious colonies? Here is a puzzle where there are many more pieces than "leaders" and "followers." Here are two complex populations, American and British, in continual flux with not only different motivations but different degrees of intensity, and different resources. Somehow out of this confused mix, the American

Revolution happened. Historians must acknowledge that the relations between causes and effects are more complicated than any simple explanations can allow.

Historians nowadays don't reject the role of the individual altogether. Biography remains the form of history most read by the general public, and biographies by their nature emphasize the individual. Still, a mood among historians sees the individual working under more complicated restraints, with more ambiguity and with both less success and less abject failure than biographers once admitted. From the Renaissance until modern times, biographers attempted to provide heroes to be imitated or villains whose examples were to be shunned. Now the emphasis is less judgmental, more dispassionate, more balanced—although on occasion this or that historian can still erupt in moral indignation at past wrongs.

Historians now study sources and deal with issues that once drew little attention at all. For centuries the writing of history was almost entirely about what men did. If women entered the story, it was because they did things male historians generally expected men to do. They ruled countries, as did Queen Elizabeth I of England; they refined radium, as Marie Curie did in France; they wrote novels, as many women have done for several centuries—some like George Eliot in England and George Sand in France, using male pseudonyms to gain acceptance. Now historians are turning to many other areas of historical interest. A random glance through recent issues of the *AHR* will show titles such as Elizabeth Heineman's "The Hour of the Woman: Memories of Germany's 'Crisis Years' and West German National Identity."[7] And we have books such as the study of Asunción Lavrin, *Women, Feminism, and Social Change in Argentina, Chile, and Uruguay, 1890–1940*,[8] a work that studies the

---

[7] Elizabeth Heineman, "The Hour of the Woman: Memories of German's 'Crisis Years' and West German National Identity," *American Historical Review* (April 1996): 354–395.

[8] Asunción Lavrin, *Women, Feminism, and Social Change in Argentina, Chile, and Uruguay, 1890–1940* (Lincoln: University of Nebraska Press, 1995).

history of feminism in three South American countries. These are topics that would have made conventional male historians of a century ago tremble in horror, but today they occupy an honored and fascinating place in serious research. In a similar way historians such as John Thornton, in his *Africa and Africans in the Making of the Atlantic World, 1400–1680,*[9] study the role of people of African descent in many societies, while still others write of the history of immigrants, labor history, sexual history, the history of fashion, the history of sports. All these and more demonstrate interests of historians toiling to uncover as much of the human experience as possible and leading the profession of history itself away from the notion that to understand the past we need only understand the personalities and decisions of a few white male leaders.

Whatever its subject, the study of history is an unending detective story. Historians try to solve mysteries in the evidence and to tell a story that will give order to the confusion of data we inherit from the past. Historians make connections, assign causes, trace defects, make comparisons, uncover patterns, locate dead ends, and find influences that continue through the generations until the present. And in doing so they apply their minds to the sources and their considered judgments to the evidence, writing those stories about the past they intend to be both credible and true.

We, then, encounter history by reading and by our own writing. We read books and articles, and slowly we gain some understanding of the shape of the past, the general framework within which events took place. When we study history in college, we write about the past using the methods of professional historians. Writing helps us think about what we know, and of course it helps our instructors see what we know and how we think.

This little book will guide you through some major steps in writing papers in history for college undergraduate classes. It is a book both about methods in historical study and about methods in

---

[9] John Thornton, *Africa and Africans in the Making of the Atlantic World, 1400–1680* (Cambridge: Cambridge University Press, 1992).

writing. It should help you gain some understanding of general problems underlying all historical study, and it should help your writing in all courses that you take in college or university. It should also make you a better detective and a better teller of some of the innumerable stories that, taken together, make up the study of the past.

Most of the book will deal with research you can conduct in your own college library or on the Internet. A brief section will also explain how to take notes and how to use those notes to do well on both research papers and on exams you may take in a history course.

THE ESSAY IN HISTORY

■ ■ ■

As we wrote in the introduction, history is far more than an assembly of facts. It is the writer's interpretation of facts that raises questions, provokes curiosity, and makes us ask the questions *who*, *what*, *where*, *when*, and *why*. The writer's interpretation adds up to what is called a "thesis," a point of view that binds everything in an essay together.

In this chapter, we suggest ten principles to help you study your own writing about history to see if it conforms to the expectations readers of history bring to books and articles. Readers typically bring to your writing expectations they have formed by reading other books and articles about history. Don't disappoint them. Guide your own work by the following standards.

1. Good historical essays have a sharply focused, limited topic.

You can develop a thrill of discovery *only* if your topic is sufficiently limited to let you study and think about the sources carefully. If you are able to choose your own topic, select one you can manage in the time and space you have available. Sometimes your instructor may assign a topic for your essay. Usually, such prescribed topics are already sharply focused, but even if they are not you can usually find ways to limit the essay you prepare.

Most unsuccessful history papers, in our experience, fall short because the writer presents a subject no one can possibly treat in a paper of the sort generally required in undergraduate history courses. Several years ago, an 18-year-old student of ours wanted to write a psychoanalysis of Henry VIII—in seven pages! England's Henry VIII was a complex and unpleasant man, as any one of his six wives as well as numerous courtiers might have testified. If a modern psychiatrist with degrees in medicine and psychotherapy put Henry on the couch and interviewed him week after week, two or three years would pass before the psychiatrist would feel capable of making a judgment about Henry's character and motives. A student with no training in psychiatry and no more than limited knowledge of the thousands of pages written about this complex and frequently ruthless king cannot say anything worthwhile on so broad a topic, and certainly not in such a brief essay.

Here is a lesson to brand in fire across any young historian's mind: If you try to do too much, you will not do anything. To write a good essay in history you must be sure that evidence is available, that you have time to study it carefully and repeatedly, and that you choose a topic on which you can say something worthwhile. Some of our students have written papers such as these: "A Study of the Prejudices against Blacks and Women in the 1911 Edition of the *Encyclopaedia Britannica*"; "The Impact of John H. Harris's History, *A Century of Emancipation*, on British Twentieth-Century Anti-Slavery Policies"; "How a Confusion in Orders Caused the British Disaster in the Battles of Lexington and Concord on April 19, 1775," and "A Study of the Causes of Food Riots in Eighteenth-Century France." All of these papers depended on sources the writers could study carefully in the time available before the papers were due.

It is always a good idea to discuss paper topics with your instructor. Sometimes a brief conversation can sharpen a topic so that your paper will become a genuine exploration of an interesting subject. Or you may be able to discern a more focused approach to a topic your instructor has assigned. In either case, it is important that you write a good title for your essay, one that represents the contents of the essay as clearly as possible. And from a clear title, it will be easier to move quickly to the purpose of your paper. Remember: The title not only helps your reader know what you are talking about; it also helps you to be certain you have defined a subject clearly.

2. Historical essays should have a clearly stated argument.

Historians write essays to interpret something they want readers to know about the past. They provide data—information from sources as well as other evidence—and their argument about what the facts mean.

"Argument" here does not mean angry, insulting debate as though anyone who disagrees with you is a fool. Rather, it is the main thing the writer wants to tell readers, the reason for writing the essay. It is the thesis of the paper, the proposition that the writer wants readers to accept. A good historical essay quietly expresses the thrill of a writer's discovery. You cannot have that thrill yourself or convey it to others if you do nothing but repeat what others have said about your topic. Don't be content with telling a story others have told hundreds of times, the sort of story you might copy out of an encyclopedia whose aim is to give you the facts, the facts, and nothing but the facts. Find something puzzling in the evidence, and try to solve the puzzle or to explain why it is a puzzle. Ask a question, and try to answer it. But get to the point straightaway.

A good essay sets the scene quickly, reveals a tension to be resolved, and sets out in the direction of a solution. Some writers take so long to introduce their essays that readers lose interest before they get to the writer's real beginning. Some writers shovel out piles of background information or long accounts of previous scholarship in a somewhat frantic effort to prove that the writer has studied the issue. Or they may give some sort of moral justification for the topic, implying something like this: "I am writing this paper to make a better world and to prove that I am on the right side." The best writers have something to say and start saying it quickly. Readers should know your general subject in the first paragraph, and within two or three paragraphs they should usually know why you have written your essay and the argument you wish to make.

Often an apt quotation from a source provides a launch pad that allows the writer to get quickly into the subject at hand. Look at the quotation from a Chinese Emperor that historian Joanna Waley-Cohen uses in her article, "China and Western Technology in the Late Eighteenth Century," and how she uses it to introduce her subject:

"We have never valued ingenious articles, nor do we have the slightest need of your country's manufactures."

Having begun with this quotation, Professor Waley-Cohen proceeds with her essay:

By the late eighteenth century, the balance of European opinion had tilted against China. Westerners, earlier in the century almost uncritical in their admiration, came to the conclusion that the Chinese seemed unwilling, or unable, to improve on their earlier inventions, such as gunpowder and the compass, which formed part of the foundation for Western development. The famous assertion of Chinese self-sufficiency quoted above, made in 1793 by the Qianlong emperor (r. 1736–1795) in response to Lord Macartney's embassy from King George III, seemed to epitomize Chinese aloofness to the potential offered by Western knowledge.

Europeans especially equated this apparent lack of interest in what the West had to offer with a lack of interest in science and practical technology, because at that time the West had come to define itself in terms of, and derive a strong sense of superiority from, its undoubted technological power. From such a perspective, it was an easy step to regarding the Chinese as inferior in an overall sense. These views took firm hold as the nineteenth century unfolded and have remained tenacious to this day. Although scholars have recently exploded the myth of China's "opposition" to Western science, it remains widely believed, and, in the case of technology, neither the conviction of the Chinese lack of interest or the assumptions on which it rested have been subjected to serious inquiry.

Yet the situation in the eighteenth century was far more complex than Qianlong's public declaration suggests. In the preceding decades, he and a number of others in China had displayed considerable interest in all manner of things Western, particularly science and technology. Although this interest was duly recorded by a range of Western observers and made widely available to their European readers, the overwhelming body of opinion disregarded that evidence in favor of the attitudes outlined above.[1]

---

[1] Joanna Waley-Cohen, "China and Western Technology in the Late Eighteenth Century," *American Historical Review*, 98(1993): 1525–1526.

You can tell from this opening that Professor Waley-Cohen will attack the standard opinion about China and technology, and so she does. Try to be as direct as she is.

Once you have begun, don't digress. Stick to the point. Be sure everything in your paper serves your main purpose, and be sure your readers understand the connection to your main purpose of everything you include. Don't imagine that you have to put everything you know into one essay. An essay makes a point. It is not an excuse to pour out facts as if you were dumping the contents of a can onto a tabletop.

3. Historical essays should include original thoughts of the author.

Essays are examples of reasoning. The most respected essays demonstrate an author's carefully setting things in order and making sense of them. Do not disappoint your readers by telling them only what other people have said about your subject. Try to show them that by reading your work, they will learn something new or see old knowledge in a new light, one that you have shed on the subject by your own study and thinking.

One of the saddest things we have found about teaching is the conviction of too many of our students that they have nothing fresh and interesting to say about their topics. They don't trust themselves. They cannot express a thought unless they have read it somewhere else. A reason for this lack of confidence is that some students insist on writing about large, general topics that other people have written about hundreds of times. Only a little searching will turn up evidence of topics that have seldom been written about. Such evidence exists in every college library. If you take the time to look, you too can turn up new information and shape papers that are new and original.

You may not find new facts, but you can think carefully about the facts at your disposal and come up with something fresh and interesting. You can see previously unexamined relations. You can see causes and effects and connections that others have missed. You may reflect on motives and influences. You may spot places where some sources are silent. You can present your own conclusions, which have the weight of authority behind them.

Don't write a paper in the spirit of the child who builds a model airplane bought in a kit from a hobby shop. The child sticks together parts that someone else has designed until he or she produces a model that looks like the picture on the box. While that is an achievement of sorts, it hardly compares to the simple, hand-carved airplane made by a craftsman. Some students go to the library looking for information on a broad subject like the beginnings of the Civil War and take a piece of information here and another piece there. They stick it all together without contributing anything of their own except manual dexterity. They retell a story that has been told thousands of times, and they do not present a thought that they have not read elsewhere. Why not instead read the speech Senator Jefferson Davis of Mississippi made in the United States Senate as he resigned to become president of the Confederacy? Explain in a paper his justification for secession—and see if you think he left something out. Then you have a thoughtful paper. Do not be happy until you shape a story that cannot be read in every encyclopedia or textbook in the field.

4. A good history essay conveys the same spirit of a good story.

As we said in the introduction, a good story begins with something out of balance, some tension to be received or explained. Or you can say that a good story begins with a problem. The same is true of history essays, stories about the past that are intended to be true. Here is a good beginning of such a story:

> "The whole affair was mismanaged from first to last." So wrote British Lieutenant John Barker in his diary after he survived the battles of Lexington and Concord on the first day of fighting in the American Revolution. Why did well trained professional British soldiers meet with such a disastrous defeat at the hands of disorganized

> American farmers called 'minutemen'? Barker had one answer: the ineptitude of his own British commanders.

The writer gets to the point quickly by quoting Barker and revealing a tension that the reader wants to see resolved. Seeing the quotation, a reader asks questions: "How was the affair mismanaged?" "Was Barker right?" "How could the British have avoided defeat that day?" The beginning puts various elements together, reveals tension, makes us ask questions, and proceeds. A paper on ideas can begin the same way. The writer should introduce the tension in the subject quickly—perhaps differing interpretations of an issue—and set out to explain its importance.

The main quality of any story is that it makes readers relive the experience it describes. You likely would feel cheated standing in line to be admitted to a mystery movie if a kid coming out shouts, "The girlfriend did it!" Often you will hear people say to friends who have seen a movie they plan to see, "Don't tell me how it ends." Generally you want to live through the experience for yourself. A good writer creates the experience of living through events or of living through a step-by-step interpretation of those events.

The experience of the movie, however, is not exactly like the experience of historical writing. Later on we shall suggest that when you pick up a history book to use in your research, you read the last chapter before you read the book to see where the historian is going. Still, any good piece of writing leads you through a process of discovery, providing information that lets you follow the writer's lead and arrive finally at the climax, where everything comes together. In a good essay or book about history, you can know how the story comes out and still appreciate the art of the historian in getting to that conclusion. Readers not only want to know how things come out but also how they happen.

Writers of history papers should not give surprise endings. Inexperienced writers often fall into the temptation of withholding necessary information or otherwise distracting us to prevent us from guessing where they are going. Such tactics are annoying, and professional historians do not use them. The climax in a history paper is usually a place where the last block of information is fitted in place and the writer's case is proved as well as his or her knowledge permits. The paper closes shortly after the climax because once the case is proved, a summary of the significance of the events or ideas described may be all that is necessary.

5. Historical essays are built, step by step, on evidence.

You must give readers reasons to believe your story. Your readers must accept you as an authority for the essay you present to them. You cannot write history off the top of your head, and you cannot parade your opinions unless you support them. Nobody cares about your opinions if you don't know anything or if you don't take the trouble to tell them what you do know.

Writing about history is much like proving a case in a court of law. A good lawyer does not stand before a jury and say, "My friends, I firmly believe my client is innocent. You must believe he is innocent because I say he is. I feel totally convinced that he is innocent. You may think he is guilty. I disagree. I feel in my bones that he is innocent. I want you to rule that he is not guilty because in my opinion he is not guilty. Take my word for it." Clients with such lawyers should prepare themselves to spend a long time away from home in undesirable company. A bad lawyer may repeat himself. He may shout and weep and whisper and swear to the sincerity of his feelings. But the jury will not believe him unless he can produce some evidence.

So it is with the historical essay. Your readers are judge and jury. You assume the role of the lawyer in arguing your case. It is all very good if your readers think you are sincere or high-minded or even eloquent. It is much more important that you convince them that you are right. To do that you must command your evidence and present it clearly and carefully.

What is evidence? The issue is complicated. Evidence is detailed factual information from primary and secondary sources. Primary sources are texts nearest to any subject of investigation. Secondary sources are always written *about* primary sources. Primary sources for an essay about the Mexican revolutionary Emiliano Zapata early in this century would be letters, speeches, and other writings of Zapata himself. Secondary sources would be books and articles by scholars such as John Womack and Samuel Brunk who have made careers of studying Zapata's movement and his assassination.

You must sift through all of the available sources, both primary and secondary, decide what is reliable and what is not, what is useful and what is not, and determine how you will use these sources in your work. But always keep in mind that good essays and papers are based on primary sources. Serious journalists follow a rule that historians would do well to use also: When you make a generalization, immediately support it by quoting, summarizing, or otherwise referring to a source. Generalizations are unconvincing without the help of specific information to give them context.

Historians fit their evidence together to create a story, an explanation, or an argument. To have evidence at their command, they spend days in libraries, museums, or wherever sources of evidence are to be found. You cannot manufacture evidence out of thin air; you must look for it. When you find it, you must study it until you know it almost by heart. If you make a careless summary of your evidence and get it wrong, you lose the respect of knowledgeable readers.

Our student who wanted to examine attitudes towards blacks and women in the much-praised 1911 edition of the *Encyclopaedia Britannica* had read an article in *The New Yorker* magazine about this famous edition, noted for its clear writing and careful drawings illustrating the engineering marvels of the day. The *New Yorker* article commented on the encyclopedia's racist assumptions. The student wanted to see for herself not only what the 1911 edition said about race, but how it treated women. She studied articles on the "Negro," on Africa, and on various issues relating to women, and she considered what kind of women were deemed worthy to make the pages of this work. The article in *The New Yorker* she had originally read was a secondary source; the primary source was the encyclopedia itself, and it was available in several sets in the university library.

Evidence is everywhere. Sometimes people make spectacular discoveries of lost or forgotten documents. The discovery of the journals of James Boswell, the eighteenth-century companion and biographer of Samuel Johnson, was a remarkable event. They turned up in a Scottish castle where they lay scattered about like so much waste paper. The capture of German archives following World War II was momentous, allowing historians to trace German political and military policy through this century and much of the last. The Freedom of Information Act has opened many FBI and other government files that were long secret, and more recently the collapse of the Soviet Union has opened vast archives to scholars.

The letters and papers of men and women, famous and obscure, make fascinating records of their times, and many collections have been published from the classical age to the present. Both the diary and letters of the English writer Virginia Woolf have been published in many volumes and offer an intimate view of her important career. Letters and journals make fascinating reading, especially if they cover long periods of time, and they are gold mines for the historian. You can pick a subject and follow the writer's thoughts on it, or activity in events related to the subject, and have an excellent paper for a college history course.

Sources of local history abound in courthouses, old newspapers (often preserved on microfilm), diaries, letters, tax records, city directories, the recollections of older people, and myriad other papers. These sources can provide details, often small ones, that can make the past come alive in a moment. And never forget the power of the interview in writing about history. If you write about any historical event of the past sixty or seventy years, often with a little effort you can find somebody who participated in it. Participants frequently may be delighted to share their stories with you. And their stories can illuminate major social movements in the country as a whole. Did a strike take place at a paper mill in your Maine town some years ago? Go interview some of the strikers and some mill managers to supplement what you read on the subject. Consult old newspaper and perhaps magazine files for stories about the strike that will help you ask questions.

You may also find transcripts of previous interviews in local history publications or archive collections. But always remember that in an interview, participants can get things wrong. Human beings forget, or they tell the story in such a way to exalt themselves, and sometimes they simply lie. The historian is always skeptical enough to check out the stories he or she hears, even from eyewitnesses. In doing so, you frequently will confirm that secondary sources are also essential. You should always consult books and articles written by historians about the subject you write about yourself. These books and articles will help you learn how to think about history, and they will provide much information that you can use.

Historians and their readers love evidence. They love telling details. They love old things. They immerse themselves in evidence—both primary and secondary sources—see its patterns, and write about them. To try to write a good paper without evidence is like trying to ride up a mountain on a bicycle without wheels. Of course, common sense should dictate that you consult with your instructor about your choices of evidence. And you should always take care to evaluate your sources carefully; in the next chapter we offer some suggestions about how you may do so. The confidence you develop by providing evidence for your points is only as good as the confidence your readers have in how you obtained it.

6. Good historical essays always document their sources.

Formal essays in history document their sources by means of footnotes, endnotes, or attributions written into the text. Readers want to know where you got your information. Later in this book we will discuss specifics concerning various modes of documentation. Even as you write, however, remember that you will only gain authority for your own work if you demonstrate that you are familiar with the primary sources and the work of others who have studied the same material.

Documenting sources is the best way to avoid plagiarism, and plagiarism remains the unforgivable sin of any writer. Plagiarism is the act of presenting the thoughts or words of others as your own. It constitutes the ultimate dishonesty in writing, a theft of intellectual property that is never forgiven in the publishing world. Tennessee writer Alex Haley claimed that his book *Roots* came from his investigation into the history of his own ancestors who came as slaves from Africa. The book was made into a television miniseries that gripped millions of Americans when it was aired over 12 nights in 1977. Haley was charged with plagiarism and paid $650,000 in damages to the writer whose work he had copied. Further investigation by historians revealed that he had made up much of his evidence, and when he died in 1992, his reputation among scholars was in ruins. Leading historians and writers usually ignore him, and when he is mentioned, "plagiarist" is often attached to his name. His sad example should be a warning to all writers to document their sources with care.

In colleges and universities the penalties for plagiarism are also severe. If you copy paragraphs out of an encyclopedia or another book or article, or if you don't credit ideas you have taken from other writers, and if your instructor discovers what you have done, he or she will never trust you again. You must familiarize yourself with the guidelines at your institution. Policies on plagiarism are usually stated in the college catalog. If you cannot find them, or are unclear about what they mean or how they will be applied, consult with your instructor. In many universities plagiarists are summoned before a disciplinary board and sometimes expelled for one or more terms of study, and usually the plagiarism is recorded permanently on their records. Always put material you copy from your sources in quotation marks if you use it word for word in your essay as you found it in the sources. Always tell your readers when you summarize or paraphrase a source. Always give credit to ideas you get from someone else, even if you express those ideas in your own words.

You do not have to document matters of common knowledge. Martin Luther was born on November 10, 1483. The Japanese attacked Pearl Harbor in Hawaii on Sunday morning, December 7, 1941. Zora Neale Hurston wrote the novel *Their Eyes Were Watching God*. Pieces of information like these are common knowledge. They are not disputed and are known to anyone who knows anything about these subjects.

But suppose you consider a complex topic such as the difference between a seminar and a lecture course in teaching history. You might easily find Bonnie G. Smith's 1995 *AHR* article, "Gender and the Practices of Scientific History: The Seminar and Archival Research in the Nineteenth Century."[2] If you use her data and her research on how seminars began and how they differed from the lecture courses that had gone on before them, the limitation of the historical profession to males, and the extraordinary difficulties of doing research in the nineteenth century, you must document your reliance on her work. You lose your honor and your reputation if you don't.

You may find that some ideas you get on your own are similar to those you read in secondary sources. You should then document those secondary sources and, either in a footnote or in the body of your text, point out the similarities and the differences.

7. Historical essays are written dispassionately.

Don't choke your prose with your own emotions. Historians identify with the people and the times they write about, and often in studying history emotions are aroused. In writing about the past, you judge people and decide whether they were good or bad. The best way to convey these judgments is to tell what these people did or said. You don't have to prove that you are on the side of the

---

[2] Bonnie G. Smith, "Gender and the Practices of Scientific History: The Seminar and Archival Research in the Nineteenth Century," *American Historical Review* 100(1995): 1150–1176.

angels. You can trust your reader. If characters you describe did terrible things, readers can see the evil if you give them the details. If characters did noble things, your readers can tell that, too, without any emotional insistence on your part.

Describing the British retreat from Concord and Lexington on April 19, 1775, historian Louis Birnbaum simply narrates the story:

> The mood of the British soldiers was murderous. They surged around houses along the route, instantly killing anyone found inside. Some of the regulars looted whatever they could find, and some were killed while looting by Minutemen who had concealed themselves in the houses. Houses with fires in the hearth were burned down simply by spreading the embers about. Generally, those homes without fires on the hearth escaped destruction because it was too time-consuming to start a fire with steel and flint. As the column approached Menotomy, the 23rd Regiment was relieved of rear-guard duty by the marine battalion. Colonial fire reached a bloody crescendo in Menotomy, and again British troops rushed house after house, killing everyone found inside, including an invalid named Jason Russell.[3]

The author could have said, "The criminal and bloodthirsty British soldiers acted horribly in what they did to those poor, innocent people, and these wicked British soldiers killed in the act of looting houses got what they deserved." But readers don't need such coercive comments, and they often resent them. If you present the details, you can trust your readers to have the right reactions. You waste time and seem a little foolish if you preach at them.

Good historians try to tell the truth about what happened. If you study any issue long enough and carefully enough, you will form opinions about it. You will think you know why something happened, or you will suppose that you understand someone. And you may develop strong personal views about the personalities or the outcome. Yet the evidence in history seldom stacks up entirely on one

---

[3] Louis Birnbaum, *Red Dawn at Lexington* (Boston: Houghton Mifflin, 1986), 184.

side of an issue, especially in the more interesting problems about the past. Different parts of the evidence contradict each other; using your own judgment about it all means that you must face such contradictions squarely. If you do not, knowledgeable readers may decide that you are careless, incompetent, or even dishonest.

Different historians interpret the same data in different ways. In highly controversial issues, you must take into account views contrary to your own. For example, if you should argue that Robert E. Lee was responsible for the Confederate defeat at the battle of Gettysburg in 1863, you must consider the argument of a number of historians that the blame should be laid at the feet of General James Longstreet, one of Lee's subordinates. You can still argue that Lee was the major cause of the Confederate disaster (although you should recall that the Federal army also had something to do with it). You don't weaken your argument by recognizing opposing views if you then can bring up evidence that supports your opinion against them. On the contrary, you strengthen your case by showing readers that you know what others have said, even if their opinions contradict your own. Readers will believe you if you deal with contrary opinions honestly, but they will scorn your work if you pretend that contradictions don't exist. This advice translates into a simple principle. Be honest. Nothing turns readers off so quickly as to suppose that the writer is not being fair.

Another principle is at stake here. History is not a seamless garment. Knowledge of the past—or of almost anything else—has bumps and rips and blank spots that remain even when historians done their best to put together a coherent account of it. The best plan always is to approach the study of the past with the humility that rises from the experience of ignorance.

8. The first and last paragraphs of a good history essay mirror each other.

The first and the last paragraphs of a good essay reflect some of the same words and thoughts. You can read these paragraphs and have a pretty good idea of what the intervening essay is about. An essay is somewhat like a snake biting its tail: The end always comes back to the beginning. As an example, consider the 1996 essay by Dauril Alden on "Changing Jesuit Perceptions of the Brasis During the Sixteenth Century," published in the *Journal of World History*. Professor Alden begins with this paragraph:

> During the sixteenth century, one of the most conspicuous weapons of militant Catholicism was the newly founded Society of Jesus. In many parts of Europe, its representatives served as diplomats, court preachers, confessors, and educators of the high and mighty. Throughout the empires of Spain and Portugal, Jesuits energetically confronted peoples of high and low cultures in East Asia, Southeast Asia, South Asia, Central Africa, and the Americas and encouraged them to convert to Catholicism and to adopt western modes of behavior and values. Perceiving themselves as spiritual descendants of the early apostles, the Jesuits resolutely pressed their evangelical campaigns and remained remarkably optimistic about the ultimate prospects of success of their evangelical campaigns, despite many obstacles. With the passage of time, however—as their experience among the Brasis in sixteenth-century Brazil demonstrates—their initial optimism became tempered by the realities that confronted them. Accordingly, they shifted their approach to the Amerindians from one of gentle persuasion to one that included the use of coercive measures when they deemed such steps necessary to achieve their spiritual objectives.[4]

Professor Alden goes on to tell the story of the early Jesuit missionaries in Brazil and their developing frustrations. When he comes to the end of his essay, he returns to these same themes; his final paragraph comes back to the beginning, but not in a mechanical way.

> Assuredly, the Jesuits, like their secular rivals, viewed the Amerindians through European spectacles. Like other Europeans, they were

---

[4] Dauril Alden, "Changing Jesuit Perceptions of the Brasis During the Sixteenth Century," *Journal of World History*, 3(1992): 205.

convinced that the indigenes were their cultural and moral inferiors and ought to be remolded in accordance with European norms. But the attitudes that the Jesuits and their secular rivals developed over time toward the Brasis were not significantly different from those of the English towards the Irish, Castillians toward the Guanches, the French toward the Hurons, or Anglican missionaries toward the Ukaguru of East Africa. Each dominant group was convinced of its own innate intellectual and moral superiority; each believed that it possessed a divinely ordained mission to uplift non-European inferiors; and each was blind to the cultural damage that later generations would claim that it had inflicted upon other people. The Jesuits who served in Brazil were dedicated, tireless workers in what they believed to be the Lord's vineyard, but the harvest they sought was not material gain, either for themselves or for their converts. Rather, it was a harvest of souls assured of a better world in the hereafter. That was their promise, their expectation, and the primary opportunity that drew them to hazardous missionary theaters throughout the world.[5]

Notice how the energetic Jesuits in the first paragraph become "tireless workers" in the last and how their evangelical campaigns are, at the end, referred to as a "harvest of souls." Alden effectively opens and closes his essay by giving readers a clear and consistent image of his argument. This approach is much more effective than beginning an essay by saying, "In this essay I am going to do this, this, and this," and then bringing it to an end by simply asserting, "I have done this, this, and this." Try to begin and end with more interesting statements. But however you begin, your first and last paragraphs should demonstrate some common words and thoughts.

9. History essays observe the common conventions of written English.

Sometimes student writers feel abused when instructors require them to spell words correctly, follow common practices of

---

[5] Alden, "Jesuits Perceptions," 217–218; we have removed Alden's helpful documentation on his comparative points.

grammar and punctuation in writing, and proofread their papers. But it is a terrible distraction to try to read a paper that does not observe the conventions. Readers want to pay attention to what a writer says. They do not want to ask questions like these: "Is that word spelled correctly?" "Why is a comma missing here?" "Does this word fit the context?" Reading is hard work, especially when the material is dense or complicated, as it often is in history courses. A careless attitude towards the conventions may not bother writers because they think they know what they want to say. But it throws readers off.

Students who complain when instructors enforce the conventions do themselves a great disservice. In the world beyond college, few things about your writing will be more harshly judged than careless disregard for the conventions. Most everyone would like to believe that their ideas are so compelling that no one can resist them, no matter how sloppily they write. Readers you seek to impress in a job application, a report, or a letter will judge otherwise. Later (in chapters 6 and 7) we offer some suggestions that should help you effectively express your ideas in writing. But merely reading over those suggestions, or listening to others from your instructors, is not enough. You must actively apply them.

Never hand in a paper without proofreading it carefully. Read it over and over to find misspelled words, lapses in grammar, typos, and places where you have inadvertently left out a word (a common error in these days of writing with the computer). Use the spell checker on your computer, usually an integral part of your word processing program. But remember! The computer cannot replace the brain. The spell checker can tell you when a word does not appear in the dictionary, but it cannot tell you that you should not use "there" when you mean "their" or "shot" when you mean "shut." If you also have a grammar check feature with your word processor, it will sometimes help you ask questions about your writing before your readers do. But as with the spell checker, it is not a substitute for your own careful rereading of your essay before you hand it in.

10. Historical essays speak to their intended audience.

No one can write to please or interest every possible reader. Different essays are intended for different audiences; always consider what your intended audience already knows. For most history courses, you should write for your instructor and other students who are interested in your topic but may not be specialists in the field. Define important terms. Give enough information to provide a context for your essay. Say something about your sources, but do not get lost in background information that your readers know already.

For example, if you write an interpretation of Martin Luther King, Jr.'s *Letter from Birmingham Jail* of 1965, you will bore readers and even offend them if you write as if they have never heard of Dr. King. In the same way, you don't inform your readers that Shakespeare was an English playwright or that Abraham Lincoln was president of the United States. No writer can be entirely sure what an audience knows or does not know. Just as you convey to your readers an "implied author" in what you write, you should also write with an implied reader in mind, someone you think may read your work. So the best you can do is to imagine yourself as a reader and consider the sort of thing you might read and believe, and write accordingly. But it is not always an easy task. The main principle is that you must always be making decisions about what you need to tell your readers and what you think they know already.

We tell our students that they should write their essays so fully that if their friends or spouses picked one up, they could read it with the same understanding and pleasure they might find in an article in a serious magazine. The essay should be complete in itself. The important terms should be defined. Everyone quoted or mentioned in the essay should be identified—unless someone is well known to the general public. All the necessary information should be included. Try to imagine a friend picking up an essay and not being able to stop until he or she has finished the piece. And it is always a good idea to have some other person read your work and try to say back to you what he or she thinks you have said.

These principles for a good essay should serve you well. Keep them in mind as you write your own history essays. This short, summary checklist will help you focus on them as you do.

Writer's Checklist

_____ ✔ Have I narrowed my topic sufficiently?

_____ ✔ Do I have a clearly stated argument?

_____ ✔ Are my ideas on the subject clear?

_____ ✔ Have I told a good story?

_____ ✔ Is the evidence on which I based my essay clear?

_____ ✔ Have I documented my sources?

_____ ✔ Do I write dispassionately and acknowledge other opinions?

_____ ✔ Do the first and last paragraphs of my essay mirror each other?

_____ ✔ Is my essay written clearly, using the common conventions of written English?

_____ ✔ Have I written with my intended audience in mind?

THINKING ABOUT HISTORY

■ ■ ■

Writing history involves a special way of thinking related to a subject we discussed in the last chapter—telling a story. The past in all its complexity cannot be recaptured like an instant replay in televised sports. Real life has no instant replay. History does not repeat itself. The stuff of history—human experience—moves ceaselessly, changing endlessly in a process so complicated that it is like a turning kaleidoscope that never makes the same pattern twice.

Consequently, knowing history is only possible through the stories that are told about it, stories that are told by many people, supported by many different kinds of evidence, told in different ways in different times and in different places. Indeed in many languages the words for "history" and "story" are the same. Historical research and historical thinking always involve listening to a multitude of voices, mute perhaps on the page but speaking through human intellect as you try to sort them all out and arrive at the story that is most plausible.

In modern times, a consciousness of history begins with the knowledge that present and past are different. In the past, the writing of history flourished when the historians realized that times were changing, that the new was replacing the old, and that the story of the old should be written down before it was lost. The speed of change in daily life since the coming of the industrial revolution has been extraordinary. Therefore, it should not be surprising that the interest in history has grown in proportion as change has swept the past away.

To write history means to make an effort to tell the story of the past in language that makes sense to readers in the present. But the effort to make sense to readers in the present may distort the story. It is all a very difficult business! Yet it is necessary because the past has such power. Human beings want to know how things got this way. They yearn to understand origins and purposes, and essential parts of their own lives in the present are influenced by their understanding of the past.

Not long ago debate was raised anew about the origin of an explosion that sank the U.S. battleship *Maine* in Havana Harbor in Cuba on February 15, 1898. At the time, American newspaper reports stirred public opinion to believe that the *Maine* was sunk by a bomb planted against its hull by Spanish agents. Not long afterwards the United States declared war against Spain. American troops defeated the Spaniards in Cuba, Puerto Rico, the Philippines, and other territories, and the United States acquired an overseas empire for the first time. Now some evidence seems to suggest that a fire in a coal bunker in the ship itself ignited ammunition stored nearby, sinking the ship with the loss of almost 200 American sailors. Historical research into the origins of that now distant war serves to make many people cautious when the government tells citizens today that the nation must go to war because its honor or morals are in peril if it does not. And certainly no historians after the Vietnam War tell the story of the Spanish-American war as if the United States engaged in a holy crusade against evil back then. Present and past work together to condition attitudes toward both of them.

What really happened? That is the fundamental question everyone would like to know about the past. But the problems of history resemble the problems of memory. What were you doing a year ago today? If you keep an appointment book, you can find in it the names of people you saw that day. But what did you say to each other? If you keep a journal, you have a better record. But the journal does not tell you everything. Someone says to you, "I remember when we sat on the beach at Pawley's Island, South Carolina, year before last in August and talked about Elvis Presley's death." "Oh," you may say, "I thought that was three years ago in a cafe in Charleston." You may have recorded the conversation in your journal; or you may have forgotten to make an entry that day. So where did the conversation take place?

You have sources to use to check your own memories. Historians have their sources, too, as a check against the folk history, a sort of oral tradition that gets passed down among all people to describe their past. That oral tradition, at least in predominately literate societies, usually floats in myth and legend. The sources historians use offer protection against the threat that the story of the past will be told finally by those with the loudest voices.

We have noted already that the sources for history have been conditioned by when they were created and are conditioned in the present by how they are read. Legends of the saints told in the Middle Ages are filled with miraculous happenings. St. Denis was said to have been beheaded in Paris while preaching to the pagan Gauls; he walked with his head in his hands to the site that later became the monastery of St. Denis outside the city, and he set his head down there to mark the place where he should be buried. The kings of France were later buried in the monastery church built on the site. A statue of the saint, holding his head in his hands, stands now on the front of Notre Dame Cathedral in Paris. (It is a reconstruction of a statue torn down by mobs in the French Revolution.)

Most of us don't believe that people walk about holding their severed heads in their hands. You respect this tale as a charming legend, not literal truth. Did the people of medieval Paris believe the story of the miracle? In a supremely reasonable attitude toward the past, you may assume that the story of St. Denis was a good way for the bishops of Paris to emphasize the importance of their city and the truth of the orthodox Christian theology they professed. Paris achieved a sacred status because of the miracle. But who can tell? Maybe the bishops did believe the story, and perhaps you have to revise your nice, reasonable explanations for its origins.

And what happens when applying nice, reasonable explanations to a modern phenomenon such as Adolf Hitler? How could Hitler take over Germany? He devised a mad and passionate hatred of Jews and created in the Holocaust one of the great horrors of Western history. Could he do so because the Germans were historically more anti-Semitic than other European peoples and were waiting for someone like himself to put their hatred of the Jews into a program to exterminate them? Or was anti-Semitism a hateful virus infecting all European countries (and the United States), and did a collection of historical accidents bring Hitler to power and create the Holocaust? Could similar accidents have happened in other European countries so that any one of them might have been capable of the genocide that Hitler and the Germans imposed on the Jews? Debate on this issue has recently raged furiously in historical books and journals and in the popular press.

The stories historians tell are about human beings living in particular times and places. Human motives are in every age complex, mysterious, and often absurd. Many people in every land do crazy and destructive things for what seems to be no reason, and scapegoats for national calamities or imagined enemies are summoned up by hysterical leaders to be blamed and to have horror inflicted upon them. "Rational" people cannot believe St. Denis walked across Paris carrying his severed head in his hands. But how could "rational" people also acquiesce in Hitler's plans for Germany?

All this is to say that history involves you in modes of thought common to daily life as well as in the effort to understand acts and ideas utterly foreign to your own. You must weigh evidence, deciding what to believe and what not, what you know and what you think is probable or at least plausible. Historians tell stories about what happened. They try to discover what it all means—and in so doing try to understand better what it is to be a human being. You will begin to think creatively in the study of history by questioning your sources.

QUESTIONING SOURCES

Good history papers are built on primary sources, but secondary sources are essential to the historian's task, and you should always

use them. The trick is not to follow slavishly the materials you find
in secondary sources. Use them to add to your own knowledge and
to help you shape your own questions about the material. As you
read keep, key these familiar questions in mind—*who, what, when,
where,* and *why*—as your guide; jot those questions down in your
notes and to try to answer them briefly as you read. They will help
you sort things out and organize your approach to the topic you are
writing about. These questions correspond to an almost universal
way that literate people respond to information, and they have long
been used by historians in working with sources. When they focus
on something that happened, historians ask who the people involved were, what exactly happened, when it happened, where, and
why. The answers often overlap. It may be impossible to separate a
what question from a *why* question. To explain what happened is
sometimes to explain why it happened. And you can scarcely separate a *who* question from a *what* question. To talk about someone is
to discuss what that person did.

The overlap of questions is the very reason they are so useful in
research. A complex event is like an elaborate tapestry tightly woven
of many different-colored threads. The threads are distinct, but they
are hard to sort out. These questions help keep your eyes on this
or that important thread so you can see how it contributes to the
whole. They will help immeasurably in analyzing human actions.
The emphasis you place on one question or another may determine
the approach you take to writing an essay about a historical event.
And thus the focus of your questioning may alter the problems you
identify and the story you will tell. Remember that each question
can be posed in many different ways. There is not one *who* question
or one *what* question or one *why* question. There may be dozens.
Ask as many of them as you can. Push your mind.

These research questions can frequently help you work
through the malady referred to as writer's block. All writers experience this affliction at one time or another. You cannot get started,
cannot go on, or cannot finish. If you write out each of the questions
and various answers to them, you can give your mind a push that

starts an engine going in your head. Writing stimulates the mind; we cannot emphasize that point enough. Almost any process that makes you write about the topic of your essay will fill your mind with thoughts you could not have had if you had not started writing first.

"Who" Questions

Many historical topics center on individuals. If your topic is one of these, you will want to begin with *who* questions. Who was Pearl S. Buck? Whom did she write about? Who loved her work? Who were some of her critics? Who was influential in interpreting her work? As you ask such questions while reading your sources, keep a record of them and jot down the answers—or note that you don't know the answers. You should also recognize a multitude of other questions which occur as you do this. Where did she live in China? What did her missionary experience there contribute to her view of that country? What did she do to influence American attitudes towards China? Why did she win the Nobel Prize? When was the prize given to her? What did literary critics say about her work? What did her fans say about her? What do people say about her work now? When did the attitude about her work begin to change? Why did it change? All these will take you to still other sources.

As you ask—and answer—these additional questions, your thought evolves. You begin to see relations between some of your questions. For example, you may push yourself to ask a dozen or more *where* questions or a multitude of *why* questions. And you may begin to read some of your sources differently. For example, you likely know that the American public was shocked when the Communists under Mao Zedong took over the Chinese mainland in 1949. Many politicians, including Senator Joseph McCarthy of Wisconsin, claimed that the United States had "lost" China for democracy because the U.S. Department of State was infested with Communist agents. Now such talk seems silly at best and malicious at worst. Did Pearl Buck's idealistic books about China, especially her classic *The Good Earth*, help create an unreal impression of the situation there? Questions such as these can lead you to read—or perhaps reread—Buck's books, reviews of her work written in her own time, and to articles written about her since. From them you can find your way to a good essay. And your initial *who* questions will have opened the door to your essay.

"What" Questions

What questions, of course, have their basis in the fundamental problem for historical understanding. What happened? But as you probe your sources, asking *what* questions may involve weeding out legends and misunderstandings to see what really happened. A frequent question which will come to mind as you read your sources is, "What does this mean?" Often you will be trying to see what people in the past meant by the words they used. These meanings can confuse us because they often change.

In the nineteenth century, the word "liberal" was used to describe businessmen who wanted to make a place for themselves in a country ruled by an aristocracy with its power based on land. The liberals were capitalists who thought government ought to keep its hands off business. Most liberals believed that the economy ran by implacable laws of supply and demand and that any effort to help working people interfered with those laws and was bound to lead to catastrophe.

In the twentieth century, the word "liberal" was used by Americans to describe those who want government to hold the balance of power between the strong and the weak, the rich and the poor. At the beginning of the twenty-first century, neither major American political party wants to use the word because it implies spending by the government for programs to help the poor and the weak, and consequent taxes to support that spending.

What relations exist between the use of the words in these different ways? Liberals in both the nineteenth and twentieth centuries have advocated "liberty," the root word of liberal. Nineteenth-century liberals wanted to create liberty for the business classes who suffered under custom that gave political power to landed aristocrats. Twentieth-century liberals have tried to create more liberty for the poor, including the liberty to have a public school education with its recognition of talent and opportunities for advancement. What changed in American life to account for the difference in the concept of liberty? And what brought about the shift in attitudes toward the words "liberal" and "liberalism"?

When you use such broad terms in your writing, you must define what you mean by them. Be on guard against reading today's definition into yesterday's words. Do not rely on simple dictionary definitions. Words are defined by their context in time and place, and you must be sure to understand what they mean in their original context.

"When" Questions

Sometimes you know exactly when something happened: the moment the first Japanese bombs fell on Pearl Harbor, the moment Franklin Roosevelt died, and exactly where the Confederate charge reached its high-water mark on the third day of the battle of Gettysburg. Of course, this certainty is born of our acceptance of a common system of measuring time. Historians know this has not always been the case, and to some extent it is not the case today. The Islamic method of reckoning time, for example, is based on different initial assumptions—the *hijrah* (or flight) of Mohammed from Mecca to Medina, rather than the birth of Jesus—and a different method— lunar rather than solar—of calculating the passage of days. The history of calendars is itself a fascinating subject of historical study. Nonetheless, historians generally accept the western, or Gregorian, method of time calculation to avoid confusions, and it has been a practical and realistic way to answer many *when* questions.

But asking when something happened in relation to something else can provide a fascinating topic of research. When did Israel leave Egypt in the Exodus described in the Bible? Several dates have been argued. Different dates mean different chronologies for Israel's relations with other nations in the region and for the development of

Israel's history. When did volcanic eruptions destroy Minoan civilization on Crete? The question is related to the rise of power on the Greek mainland under states such as Athens and Sparta. When did Richard Nixon first learn that members of his White House staff were involved in the Watergate burglary of June 17, 1972? "When did you know" became an important question put to Nixon and his aides in the subsequent investigations. That question has come to epitomize a skeptical approach to historical sources, and one you would do well to adopt in your research.

"Where" Questions

Questions about where things happened can often be absorbing. No one knows exactly the location of the Rubicon River. Julius Caesar crossed it with his army in violation of a law of the Roman Republic that forbade the army to approach the capital. But wherever it was, it has another name today. The Rubicon was in northern Italy and formed the border between the Roman province known as Cisalpine Gaul and the Roman Republic itself. But which modern Italian river was then called the Rubicon is a matter of dispute. Deciding where the Rubicon was, however, might help historians understand how much warning the Roman Senate had when Caesar moved with his troops on the capital.

Where questions involve geography, and you should think about geography when you write. Geography may not yield anything special for your work, but if you ask the right questions, geography may open a door in your mind onto a hitherto unimagined landscape of events and explanation. The Annales school of history in France made geography one of its fundamental concerns, asking such questions as how long it took to travel from one place to another in Europe, what the major trade routes were, where different crops were grown, and what cities had the closest relations to one another. For all historians, a good topographical map showing roads, rivers, mountains, passes, coasts, and locations of towns remains an indispensable resource. Using such a map, you will be able to ask better questions about your sources.

"Why" Questions

Sometimes you know what happened. But basic curiosity should lead you to ask: why did it happen? Why did it have the influence it did? These questions—essentially about cause and effect—create an eternal fascination. But cause and effect are like unruly twins. In historical study they are inseparable, yet it is often difficult to see just how they relate to each other. Thinking about such *why* questions should lead you to keep in mind the following considerations about one of the most important topics in the study of history—cause and effect.

1. Always distinguish between the precipitating cause and the background causes of a great event.

You might call the precipitating cause the triggering cause, the cause that sets events in motion. The background causes are those that build up and create the context within which the precipitating cause works. Precipitating causes are often dramatic and fairly clear. Background causes are more difficult to sort out and often ambiguous.

The precipitating cause of the Civil War was the bombardment and capture of Fort Sumter by the forces of South Carolina on April 12, 1861. No one would claim that the incident in Charleston Harbor all by itself caused the Civil War. Behind the events of that Friday morning were many complex differences between North and South. These were background causes of the war, and ever since, historians have been trying to sort them all out to tell a sensible and precise story to explain why America's bloodiest war occurred.

Background causes offer rich possibilities for writing about the *why* of history. They allow writers opportunities for research, analysis, and conjecture. But precipitating or triggering causes can be worthwhile subjects in themselves. Exactly what happened at Fort Sumter on that April day in 1861? Why were passions so aroused on that particular day in that particular year? The *what* question and the *why* question come together—as they often do.

2. Remember that historical causation is complex.

It is almost always a mistake to lay too much responsibility for a happening on only one cause. Good historical writing considers how many different but related influences work on what happens. Causes in history are like the tributaries to a great river. While a bad historian sees only the main channel of the largest stream, a good historian looks at the entire watershed and maps the smaller streams that contribute to the whole.

Good historians see things in context—often a large context of people and events surrounding what they seek to describe. Thinking in context means you try to sort out and weigh the relative importance of various causes when you consider any important happening. Nineteenth-century historians thought that if they understood the leaders, then they knew everything they needed to know about historical movements. But in the twentieth century, historians discovered the common people who must follow if others are to lead. As a result, more historians are now asking questions such as: Why did a rebellion of Indian soldiers in the service of the East India Company in 1857 in Bengal lead to massacres of British settlers all over India? Why were the British able to persuade other Indians to unite with them to put down the rebellion in horrifying atrocities committed on the rebels and their supporters? These questions lead to investigations of mass culture, including the lives of people often scarcely literate who have left few written records behind. Since it is hard to resurrect the life of the masses, the problem of answering the *why* questions of history becomes complex and uncertain. But these difficulties don't remove from historians the obligation to try to make sense of them.

3. Be cautious in your judgments.

Do not give easy and simple causes for complex and difficult problems. Do not argue that the Roman Empire fell only because Romans drank water from lead pipes or that the South lost the Civil War only because Lee was defeated at Gettysburg. These events were caused by complex influences. It is foolish trying to lay too much responsibility on one dramatic event or famous leader.

The caution should also extend to your judgments about motivation in history. The Roman Emperor Constantine legalized Christian worship in the Roman Empire after about 313 A.D. Was he a sincere Christian? Or did he see that the Christians were numerous and possessed a strong organization that might help hold together his decaying empire? Was he devout? Or was he cynical? Historians have come down on both sides.

Some *why* questions may seem to have been answered. Yet an inquiring historian may look on the evidence again and discover another possible answer that contradicts accepted wisdom. Why did the South suffer so much poverty in the years after the Civil War? An earlier answer was "Reconstruction," the supposedly merciless exploitation of the South by carpetbaggers from the North. Now the prevailing opinion is that white Southerners themselves—with their one-crop economy, their resolve to suppress black citizenship, and their unwillingness to support public education—were responsible for many of their own difficulties. Realizing that careful study of the evidence may often turn up new possibilities about questions that seem to have been answered should be motivation enough for caution. There are other reasons to do so, of course, and many relate to the problem of historical reasoning.

4. Avoid common historical fallacies.

"A fallacy is not merely an error itself," historian David Hackett Fischer observed a number of years ago, "but a way of falling into error. It consists in false reasoning, often from true factual premises, so that false conclusions are generated."[1] In his book on the subject, Professor Fischer suggested quite a number of specific fallacies—and offered examples of each from historical writing. For several

---

[1] David Hackett Fischer, *Historians' Fallacies: Toward a Logic of Historical Thought* (New York: Harper and Row, 1970), xvii.

years after his book appeared, historians scanned its pages hoping not to find their names included! Far better, though, simply to keep a few of the most common errors in mind so that you might avoid them in your writing. You may find it both fascinating and instructive to review some of the many examples of historical fallacies that Professor Fischer offers in his book. Here we will only mention two of them which we have, too frequently, observed in student writing.

You may be familiar with the term *straw man*. People set up straw men when they argue against positions their opponents have not taken or when, without evidence, they attribute bad motives to opponents. Such arguments may be easily attacked, and so give the appearance of victory—except that they are beside the point. Avoid the temptation. You should also eschew the easy assumption that because many historians agree on an issue, they must be right. Consensus by experts is not to be scorned, but experts can also be prone to prejudices.

By all means avoid the fallacy that comes wearing an elaborate Latin name—*post hoc, ergo propter hoc*, "After this; therefore because of this." It refers to the fallacy of believing that if something happens after something else, the first happening caused the second. A more subtle problem with this fallacy arises with events that are closely related, although one does not necessarily cause the other. The New York stock market crashed in October 1929. The Great Depression followed. But it is a mistake to say that the crash caused the Depression; both seem to have been caused by the same economic forces. When you confront this sort of relation in writing essays, it is necessary to think out the various strands of causation and to avoid making things too simple.

MAKING INFERENCES

In our discussion of how you might question your sources, we have assumed the ability of the mind to infer. Humans manage their daily lives by making inferences. If in the morning you see low, dark clouds piled in the sky, when you leave home, you take along an umbrella. Why? You have seen such clouds before, and they have often meant rain. You infer by calling on past experience to interpret a present event or situation. You cannot always be certain that what you infer is true. Sometimes black clouds blow away quickly, leaving the skies clear so that you lug around a useless umbrella and maybe a raincoat all day long. But without inference humans would have to reinvent the world every morning.

Historians infer some answers to all of their questions. They strive to make sense of a document, of other evidence, or of inconsistencies between several sources. They try to decide exactly what is reliable and to understand why the evidence was created, when it might have been, where, and by whom. The aim of inference is coherence. Historians try to fit everything they know into a plausible whole. For example, you would likely infer that there is something fishy about documents that use words not coined until long after the purported age of the document itself. Suppose you read this sentence in the diary of a pioneer woman who supposedly crossed the plains on her way to California in 1851: "We are having a very hard time, and I know that Americans who drive through Nebraska in years to come on Interstate 80 will scarcely imagine what we have endured." You would immediately infer that something is seriously wrong with the claims of this document!

In practice, historians face similar problems in dealing with all sorts of evidence. This is particularly true where the written documents are missing, prove not very helpful, or seem to be inconsistent. But that does not keep a good historian from asking questions, and making inferences, in trying to tell a true story about the past. After reading accounts of Hernando De Soto's sixteenth-century journey through what is now the southeastern United States, Alfred W. Crosby was struck by the inconsistencies between those descriptions and the accounts of the first intended settlers two centuries later:

> In eastern and southern Arkansas and northeastern Louisiana, where De Soto found thirty towns and provinces, the French found only a handful

of villages. Where De Soto had been able to stand on one temple mound and see several villages with their mounds and little else but fields of maize between, there was now wilderness. . . .

In the sixteenth century, De Soto's chroniclers saw no buffalo along their route from Florida to Tennessee and back to the coast, or if they did see those wonderful beasts, they did not mention them—which seems highly improbable. Archeological evidence and examination of Amerindian place names also indicate there were no buffalo along the De Soto route, nor between it and salt water. A century and a half later, when the French and English arrived, they found the shaggy animals in at least scattered herds from the mountains to the Gulf and even to the Atlantic. What had happened in the interim is easy to explain the abstract: An econiche opened up, and the buffalo moved into it. Something had kept these animals out of the expanse of parklike clearings in the forest that periodic Amerindian use of fire and hoe had created. That something had declined or disappeared after 1540. That something was, in all likelihood, the Amerindians themselves, who naturally would have killed the buffalo for food and to protect their crops.

The cause of that decline and disappearance was probably epidemic disease. No other factor seems capable of having exterminated so many people over such a large part of North America.[2]

Crosby's questions led him to seek additional information—in this case from ecology and geography—and then arrive at an answer on the basis of probable inference. Similar examples of inference abound in the writing of history on any subject. The French medievalist Jacques Le Goff has classified the standing of various jobs in the Middle Ages by noting jobs that the church refused to allow priests to hold. If a priest could not hold the job, Le Goff reasoned, it must be work generally scorned. He mentioned the jobs of innkeepers, owners of bathhouses, and jugglers, among others.

Many scholars also use wills and similar legal documents as points of inference. Wills bequeathing possessions show what the maker of the will owned, and that information can in turn suggest a

---

[2] Alfred W. Crosby, *Ecological Imperialism: The Biological Expansion of Europe, 900–1900* (Cambridge: Cambridge University Press, 1986), 212–213. We have eliminated Crosby's citation of his considerable evidence.

great deal about the life that the person lived. Wills can show other things as well. In England, for example, historians may get some indication of the degree of orthodox Catholic sentiment in the sixteenth century by looking at the religious formulae expressed in wills. If they find formulae mentioning the Virgin Mary and the saints, they infer strong Catholic sentiment. If they have formulae that mention only God and Christ, they infer some form of Protestantism.

The laws of any society also provide a rich field for inference. Laws don't come out of thin air. They reflect the values of the people who make them, and they respond to conduct that runs counter to values in that society in that time. Laws are not made by just anybody, but by people with some kind of authority—economic, religious, military, or whatever. Usually the people who make laws can enforce their values on everyone else—but not always. You can infer the nature of authority by looking at laws and can see conduct that rulers assume runs against those values. By comparing laws and legal cases that come to the courts, historians can often infer how strictly laws are enforced. Most cities and states have laws against littering, but not many citizens end up in court for throwing beer cans out the windows of cars on our highways. You may infer that the authorities think littering is bad, but not bad enough to punish those who litter.

When you make an inference important to your study of the sources, you become a questioner. You don't read your sources passively. You read them actively, trying to fill in the gaps you always find in them. And in the process, you should also be assessing their value in helping you tell the story about the past you want to write.

EVALUATING MATERIALS

This evaluation process is, of course, essential to historical writing. All historians, in one way or another, engage in making assessments of the materials they use in crafting their histories. They have often referred to these practices as the "critical method," a key part of their special way of thinking. Based on long experience, historians divide this approach into two parts, what they call "external criticism" and "internal criticism."

External criticism is basically an effort to determine if the documents they are using are, in fact, genuine—that they are what they purport to be. For centuries in the Middle Ages, people believed that a document called the Donation of Constantine had been written by the Emperor Constantine early in the fourth century when he became a Christian. According to the document, Constantine was cured of leprosy by a pope, and in gratitude moved from Rome to Constantinople and gave rule in the West to the pope and his successors. The document was used to prove the superiority of popes over kings in Europe.

In the fourteenth century, an Italian named Lorenzo Valla began to ask some questions about the Donation. Why did none of the people around Constantine who wrote about him and his reign mention his attack of leprosy or the Donation? Why did the document use words that were not coined until centuries later? Why was it not quoted by anyone until about the ninth century? Why did it make many historical errors? Valla inferred the work could not have referred to an actual historical event and that it could not have been written in the time of Constantine. Therefore he concluded that the work was a forgery, and his judgment has been accepted ever since.

But the record of counterfeit historical documents is not limited to those created centuries ago. There are a number of well known and more recent examples of primary sources which were not what they seemed to be. One involves the fascinating story of Sir Edmund Backhouse, an eccentric English orientalist, described by historian Hugh Trevor-Roper as *The Hermit of Peking*. Backhouse had long been considered a leading scholar of early twentieth century Chinese history. His reputation rested on his command of the Chinese language and the good fortune to have discovered a number of important documents that served as the basis of his writings. He was also a benefactor of the Bodleian Library at Oxford University, donating some of those manuscripts—and a large number of others—to its China collections. He also penned a long memoir which, almost thirty years after his death in 1944, also was to find its way to the Bodleian. But because his biographical reflections were considered by many who saw them to be—even by the quietly permissive English upper class standards of his own time—somewhat obscene, Bodleian officials asked Trevor-Roper, Regis Professor of Modern History at Oxford, to analyze them. In doing so, he produced a sort of literary biography concluding Backhouse was not an extraordinarily gifted figure—unless it was as a forger! Trevor-Roper exposed the key documents Backhouse used in his best known works as the result of an elaborate hoax and the Chinese texts themselves as forgeries.

Trevor-Roper asked the obvious historian's question: Why would Backhouse perpetrate, and through his also invented memoir, try to perpetuate such a hoax? His conclusion about Backhouse's motives is revealing: "History was to him not a discipline, a means of understanding the world, but a compensation, a means of escape from it."[3] Not only does this suggest much about the man who thought this way; it also suggests something about why such a hoax might be attractive to other would-be historical pranksters. But in this case there is also an instructive sequel, one that we believe offers an incentive for caution to any writer of history.

Six years after the appearance of his book on Backhouse, Professor Trevor-Roper was drawn into another case of a disputed historical document. In April 1983, the German magazine *Stern* published excerpts from the extensive, newly discovered diaries of Adolf Hitler. As you might imagine, this caused a sensation. Were these the genuine handiwork of the Fürher himself? Many important historians were asked for their evaluation of the diaries. Drawing on his considerable experience, Trevor-Roper offered this opinion on the Hitler diaries:

> Whereas signatures, single documents, or even groups of documents can be skillfully forged, a whole coherent archive covering 35 years is far less easily manufactured.

---

[3] Hugh Trevor-Roper, *The Hermit of Peking* (New York: Alfred A. Knopf, 1977), 294.

> Such a disproportionate and indeed extravagant effort offers too large and vulnerable a flank to the critics who will undoubtedly assail it. . . . The archive, in fact, is not only a collection of documents which can be individually tested: it coheres as a whole and the diaries are an integral part of it.
>
> That is the internal evidence of authenticity.[4]

But Professor Trevor-Roper, it transpired, was actually duped by yet another clever forgery! And he was not the only one taken in by the forger, who seems to have capitalized on the widespread fascination with Hitler and the Nazis to create not just the diaries but other phony Hitler memorabilia as well. While financial gain probably was the forger's major motivation, certainly he had a similar disrespect for history as a disciplined inquiry as did Edmund Backhouse. And at least for a time, the hoax convinced even as distinguished, and skeptical, a historian as Trevor-Roper.

While his experiences should suggest that you would be well served by a healthy historical skepticism, it is unlikely you will have to make many such judgments about the authenticity of the primary sources that you use in writing your history papers. Perhaps if your sources were found in a discarded trunk or an abandoned attic, you would need to make an effort to determine if they were authentic. But many of the primary sources you are likely to employ will be found in published collections. You may reasonably expect the editors will have undertaken a careful external criticism of the documents prior to their publication. You may actually find other, unpublished primary sources in nearby archives or libraries, where the custodians of the original documents will have made such determinations. But, lest these assurances give a false sense of security, remember that you will still need to engage in the second part of the critical method: internal criticism.

---

[4] Quoted in Dave Gross, "The Hitler Diaries," *Culture-Jammer's Encyclopedia* <http://www.syntac.net/hoax/kujau.php> (n.d.; accessed 24 March 2001).

In doing so you should retain the same sense of skepticism. But you should harness that skepticism by using the techniques of asking questions and making inferences that we have already discussed. From the perspective of critical method, you can use them to help establish, first, if your sources are plausible and trustworthy, and then if they are accurate and can be corroborated. And these techniques will serve you well in dealing with secondary as well as primary sources.

Certainly the common-sense test is one of the best you have at your disposal. Historians do have to trust their own insights. They need to make reasonable judgments based on their own sense of what is possible. Does your common sense tell you that what you have read is truly plausible? Could it really have happened as your sources would have it? If your sources suggest that the Egyptian pyramids or the great stone statues on Easter Island were created by alien visitors from outer space, you have good reason to doubt them. The more fantastic the explanations you are offered, the more likely they will be little more than simple fantasy.

Yet even with a sense that the information is plausible, what leads you to trust your sources? Were those doing the reporting in a position to know what they reported? Were American veterans of the Korean War who reported that Korean civilians were indiscriminately shot actually serving in military units which were present at No Gun Re, where other Korean civilians claimed the attacks took place? Did any of them have special knowledge of the situation which would lend credibility to their testimony? Perhaps some of them served as medical corpsmen and treated the wounded. That might make their statements more trustworthy in your eyes. And in the case of secondary accounts, do they come from authors whose works have generally been considered reliable? You may have to check reviews of some historical works to help determine this.

You can also make your own determination by reading carefully to see if all of the details fit together. Are the descriptions of times and places accurate? Do the details match what is known and what can reasonably be inferred? In many British colonial territories, annual census figures remained the same year after year with no variation. District colonial administrators, it seems, did little more than make estimates and repeat them when new figures were required a year later, disregarding the improbability that births and deaths would exactly balance year after year. No historian would consider such statistics to be an accurate reflection of a region's actual population.

But for some other details it might be possible for you to seek corroborating evidence. Good historians generally try to do this, just as *Washington Post* reporters Bob Woodward and Carl Bernstein always sought other sources to confirm the details which their famous (and still unidentified) Watergate scandal informant, Deep Throat, passed on to them. Keep in mind, though, that your corroborating sources must be independent of one another if you wish to have real confidence in the accuracy of what you write. This does not mean that a single source must always be rejected. But without corroboration, you must establish through other applications of your critical methodology that your sources are accurate.

While it is true that good historians do not implicitly trust their sources, neither do they trust their own first impressions. Nor do they merely pose random questions regarding what they read, what they hear, or what they see. The exercise of the historian's critical method demands a much more systematic application of the injunctions to ask questions and make inferences. Only in doing so can you really claim to have evaluated your source materials and to have written an essay presenting a story about the past which is intended to be true. Nothing is quite so destructive to historians' reputations as presenting conclusions which do more to prove their own gullibility, laziness, or unwillingness to ask questions than to provide real insight into the meaning of the past.

As you undertake research in preparation for writing a history essay, you want always to make critical evaluations of your source materials. To make that admittedly sometimes difficult task a little easier, you might always try to keep this checklist in mind as you examine each source you discover.

Writer's Checklist

_____ ✔ On what basis can I be certain this source is genuine?

_____ ✔ Is the information truly plausible?

_____ ✔ Am I confident the source is trustworthy?

_____ ✔ Are the details contained in the source accurate?

_____ ✔ Do I have any corroborating evidence?

3

MODES OF HISTORICAL WRITING

■ ■ ■

Like other writers, historians use the four common modes of expression: description, narrative, exposition, and argument. Of these, argument is nearly always the most important mode in the college classroom, but not to the exclusion of the others. Instructors will require you to have a *thesis*, a point of view, a subject that unites your paper, a proposition you want others to believe. (*Thesis* comes from a Greek word meaning *to set down*.) Your thesis will be the argument, the reason you write the paper, the case you want to prove. In the most basic meaning of the word, though, "argument" does not mean a dispute about something. The word originally meant *to prove* or *to assert*. At an earlier time people spoke of the "argument" of a novel, meaning the novel's plot and the view of human nature and possibility that informed the writer's way of presenting the story. Even today, in written prose, argument is rather a principle of organization that unites facts and observations to present a proposition important to the writer.

But we should offer a fundamental caution: A mere collection of facts is not an essay, nor would it constitute an argument. The facts must be woven together in such a way that they support a well defined point of view that the writer wishes other people to believe. If you take notes on your reading and assemble a vast collection of historical facts about Woodrow Wilson, you don't have an essay. But if you sift through your notes and discover that Wilson often expressed negative attitudes towards black Americans, you begin to have a thesis for an essay, something you want to examine under several headings. Why did Wilson have these attitudes? What did he do in response to them? What consequences did his attitudes and his actions have? It may be that hardly any scholars have considered this aspect of Wilson's career. So when you write your own essay on the subject, you may not be arguing with anyone else. That is, you may not have a disputation or a debate with another historian on the subject. Still, your point of view is an argument.

A little later in this chapter we shall discuss argument as debate. But as you study the modes we describe below, keep in mind that in writing history papers argument—in the sense of a thesis, or a topic— is fundamental to all of the modes. The modes overlap, and you may use all of them in a single paper; certainly we have in our own writing. A narrative paragraph may tell how British troops ferried across the Back Bay of Boston on the night of April 18, 1775, were required to stand in a marsh with water up to their knees waiting for supplies they did not need, and only then tramped out to Lexington and Concord. A descriptive paragraph might give details of the marsh and the chill of an unusually cold New England spring. A brief exposition might consider the effects on tempers of having to march twelve or fifteen miles to Lexington in cold, sopping wet clothes and heavy, wet boots. A writer might then argue that the needless delay in the Cambridge marsh robbed the British of the element of surprise and led to their humiliating defeat at the hands of the American minutemen in the battles that began the Revolutionary War.

Although the four modes often overlap, they are distinct; one will usually predominate in a given book or essay. When you write an essay, try to determine which modes will best advance your argument. If you have a clear idea of the mode best suited to your purposes, you make the task easier for both you and your readers.

DESCRIPTION

Description presents an account of sensory experience—the way things look, feel, taste, sound, and smell—as well as more impressionistic descriptions of attitudes and behavior. Popular history includes vivid descriptions, and you can describe people and places with great effect in a paper intended for a college or scholarly audience. No matter how learned or unlearned in the limitless facts of a historical period, everyone has had sensory experiences similar to those of people in the past. Senses are the common denominator in human life. Perhaps as a consequence of reliance on sensory experience and observations, readers like concrete details about physical reality in books and articles about history. Details reassure your readers that the world of the past was enough like their own world to imagine it, to place themselves within it (for at least a moment), and to find it familiar and understandable.

Few historical papers are devoted to description alone, and it is seldom useful to try to describe everything. You will suffocate your essay in details. Describe only enough to kindle the imaginations of readers. In his book *Sacco and Vanzetti: The Case Resolved,* part history and part autobiography, Francis Russell tells us how he changed his mind about the celebrated trial in 1921 and execution in 1927 of Nicola Sacco and Bartolemeo Vanzetti. The two were accused of murder in a payroll robbery that took place in South Braintree, Massachusetts, on April 15, 1920. They were tried in Dedham, Massachusetts. More than forty years ago, Russell began his interest in the case by believing that they were innocent. After long and detailed study, he concluded that Sacco was guilty of murder and that Vanzetti was what in legal terminology is called an accessory after the fact. That is, Vanzetti knew Sacco was guilty but tried to help him escape the law.

The following descriptive passage sets the tone for the carefully reflective book that follows. It also has an implicit agenda intended to give readers confidence in the author of a controversial book, since received wisdom in the American liberal tradition held that Sacco and Vanzetti were innocent martyrs to Yankee New England's hatred of Italian immigrants.

> Someday, I promised myself, I was going to sit down and study the Sacco-Vanzetti trial transcript. But with the coming of the war, my interest lapsed. If I had not been called for a month's jury duty in the

Dedham courthouse in the spring of 1953, I doubt that I should ever have concerned myself with the case again. I was then living in Wellesley, eight miles away, and when the weather was good I used to walk along the back roads to Dedham. By starting at quarter to eight, I could get to the courthouse just before ten o'clock, when the morning session began.

I liked those brisk bright mornings, the earth smelling of spring, the maples in misty shades of mauve and red. From Wellesley the road dipped past the country club, curving down to Needham, a semi-suburb of repetitive three-bedroom houses, commonplace enough, yet—as I was later to discover—singularly interwoven with the Sacco-Vanzetti case.

Spring was late that year. Not until my second week, as I crossed the bridge over the Charles River the other side of Needham, did I hear the creaky notes of the red-wings among last year's cattails. A few mornings later I saw a couple of painted turtles still torpid from hibernation. From the bridge I headed up the winding road to Dedham, past much empty land, orchards, stone walls, and the driveways of discreetly hidden river estates. Then, from Common Street on Dedham's outskirts, I swung into High Street, ahead of me above the still-bare elms the courthouse dome, mosquelike in the early light, crowned by an ornate metal grille and a flagpole. On those placid mornings the flag hung limp.

It was almost a third of a century since Sacco and Vanzetti had been tried, yet the ghost of their trial still seemed to haunt the courthouse. Scarcely a day passed while I was on jury duty but some reference to it came up. It shadowed us all. We served in the same paneled room with the marble-faced clock where Sacco and Vanzetti had been tried and sentenced. There was the same enclosure for the prisoners that Sacco-Vanzetti partisans referred to as a "cage"—as if the two defendants had been exhibited like animals in a zoo. Actually, it was a waist-high metal lattice, slightly higher in the back, with nothing formidable or forbidding about it. Our white-haired sheriff, Samuel Capen, in his blue-serge cutaway, its gleaming brass buttons embossed with the state seal, and his white staff of office that he wielded like a benevolent shepherd, had been sheriff at the time of the great trial. In the overlong lunch hours he would sometimes talk about it, telling of the day Sacco and Vanzetti were sentenced, how Vanzetti made his famous speech, and how Judge Thayer sat with his head bent and never looked at him. I do not suppose any doubts had ever crossed the sheriff's mind as to the guilt of the two Italians or the rectitude of Massachusetts justice.[1]

---

[1] Francis Russell, *Sacco and Vanzetti: The Case Resolved* (New York: Harper & Row, 1986), 34–36.

Russell uses several forms of description. He makes a direct appeal to the senses as when he writes of colors ("misty shades of mauve and red"), objects ("the marble-faced clock"), sounds ("the creaky notes of the red-wings"), and smells ("the earth smelling of spring").

All these descriptions of physical reality depend on the readers' having had some experience that Russell can summon up in their memories. When he tells us that the Dedham courthouse dome looked "mosquelike in the early light," he assumes you know what a mosque is. You may not have had every experience he describes. Some readers may not have heard the "creaky notes" of red-wing blackbirds. Still these readers follow Russell's account because his description conveys authority; he has been there; he knows what he is talking about; his language conveys a familiar reality. These qualities help readers believe him.

Another kind of description here is more impressionistic, more metaphorical. Russell tells us that the enclosure where prisoners sat in the courtroom had "nothing formidable or forbidding about it." He tells us that the sheriff carried an official staff "that he wielded like a benevolent shepherd." These are his impressions. Someone else might have seen the "waist-high metal lattice, slightly higher in the back" as formidable and forbidding and might have judged that Sheriff Capen wielded his official staff like a warrior's club. Subtly, Russell has prepared you to believe his impressions because he has provided earlier vivid, benign, and believable details about his observations. He has created an "implied author"—dispassionate, warm-hearted, sharply observant—a writer you can trust. So readers are prepared to believe him also when he passes to more subjective impressionist observations, the unthreatening quality of the prisoner's "cage," the benevolence of the sheriff's flourishing his staff of office. Description often combines these two elements, the concrete and the impressionistic. They work here to prepare us to follow the author into his much more controversial belief that despite the protests that swept America when Sacco and Vanzetti were put to death, the two men were guilty.

But never make things up when you describe something. Although some readers may be entertained by flights of fancy in historical writing, historians usually find them cheap and dishonest, and with good reason. Here are two paragraphs written by the late Paul Murray Kendall in his laudatory biography of Richard III, King of England between 1483 and 1485. They describe the battle of Barnet on the morning of April 14, 1471, in which Richard, then Duke of Gloucester, fought on the side of his older brother, Edward IV, against an effort by the Earl of Warwick to overthrow King Edward.

> Suddenly there was a swirl in the mist to the left of and behind the enemy position. A shiver ran down the Lancastrian line. Exeter's men began to give way, stubbornly at first, then faster. Warwick's center must be crumbling. Richard signaled his trumpeters. The call to advance banners rang out. The weary young commander and his weary men surged forward. Then the enemy were in full flight, casting away their weapons as they ran.
>
> Out of the mist loomed the great sun banner of the House of York. A giant figure strode forward. Pushing his visor up, Richard saw that the King was smiling at him in brotherly pride. The right wing, driving westward across the Lancastrian rear, had linked up with Edward's center to bring the battle to an end. It was seven o'clock in the morning; the struggle had lasted almost three hours.[2]

Kendall's description evokes a vivid image of battle, but his scene is almost entirely made up. The sources for the battle of Barnet are skimpy. It is agreed a mist lay over the ground and that the battle was confused. In the midst of the battle, someone on the Lancastrian side shouted "treason," and others took up the cry. The Lancastrian troops in the middle of the line, thinking one of their leaders on a flank had gone over to the enemy, broke and ran. Their leader, the Earl of Warwick, was killed while trying to catch his horse. But Kendall's description of Richard meeting his brother Edward is all

---

[2] Paul Murray Kendall, *Richard the Third* (New York: Doubleday, 1965), 97.

fantasy. No wonder historian Charles Ross, in remarking on Kendall's account of Barnet, comments dryly, "The incautious reader might be forgiven for thinking that the author himself was present at the battle."[3]

Much worse than Ross's scorn is what such fictional details do to Kendall's credibility. His book aims at resurrecting the reputation of Richard III from Sir Thomas More and Shakespeare who made him a lying hypocrite and a murderer, guilty of ordering the deaths of the little sons of Edward IV after the King died. To believe such an argument against a predominant historical opinion, you must have confidence in the author. But a book so filled with fictional detail as Kendall's cannot be taken seriously by dispassionate and thoughtful readers, and it has been regularly ridiculed since its publication.

It is also important not to allow your descriptions to fall into familiar and accepted patterns of thought in an attempt to invoke what you think your reader might expect. Such an approach also runs the risk of undermining your credibility. Rather, you should tailor your descriptions to paint the mental pictures you intend to be true, ones based on the best evidence available to you. In the following paragraphs Professor Ken Wolf does this explicitly in describing the army—frequently referred to in much historical literature as a "horde"—of Genghis Khan, the great Mongol leader.

> Our word *horde*, taken from the Mongol *ordu*, meaning "camp" or "field army," suggests a huge body of dirty, undisciplined barbarians, drinking mare's blood, shooting on the run, and defeating their enemies by sheer weight of numbers. Such was not the case. Mongol armies under Genghis Khan *never* outnumbered those of their enemies; they were successful due to "splendid organization, discipline, leadership, and morale." We should add skill, for the Mongols were probably the most skilled horse soldiers of the pre-industrial age. They learned to ride their famous ponies at age three, and they began using a bow and arrow at age four or five. The adult Mongol cavalryman could shoot an arrow with

---

[3] Charles Ross, *Richard III* (Berkeley and Los Angeles: University of California Press, 1983), 21.

deadly accuracy over a hundred yards; he could do this riding full gallop and even, when necessary, retreating and shooting over his shoulder; a high saddle and stirrups (a Mongol invention later adopted in the West) kept him from falling. Mongol armies could ride for days without stopping to cook food. They carried kumis, dried milk curd, cured meat, and water and could eat, drink, and sleep on horseback. . . .

Genghis Khan used a decimal organization. Divisions, or *toumen*, of ten thousand men were divided into regiments of one thousand; these were then subdivided into squads of 100 and patrols, or *arban*, of ten men each. Each unit commander gave strict obedience to his superior, on pain of death. In campaigns, *toumens* could travel in widely separated columns and unite quickly in battle.[4]

Wolf begins with familiar images, ones that usually conjure up unpleasant thoughts of little more than groups of wild men. But then he sets about calling those stereotypes into question. He continues with much more straightforward description of Mongol soldiers, attempting to replace the unfortunate images he believes readers may hold with others which he is confident represent something closer to reality. In doing so, he is careful to avoid any explicitly evocative language, appealing instead to simple images you might well recognize from your own experiences. And when you finish reading his description of the Mongol cavalrymen, you likely will better understand the argument which is the foundation of his essay.

When you write descriptive passages in your essays, always consider these questions:

Writer's Checklist

- ✔ Do my descriptions reflect sensory experience?
- ✔ Are the descriptions relevant to my essay's purpose?
- ✔ Are the impressions and emotions I evoke common enough to be recognizable?

---

[4] Ken Wolf, "Genghis Khan: Incomparable Nomad Conqueror," in *Personalities & Problems: Interpretive Essays in World Civilizations*, 2nd ed. (Boston: McGraw-Hill College, 1999), 2:91–92; we have removed Wolf's footnotes.

_____   ✔ Have I based my descriptions on sound evidence?
_____   ✔ Have I avoided stereotypical descriptions in favor
        of more accurate ones?

NARRATIVE

As important as both making a point and providing clear descriptions are, narratives tell stories, and stories are the bedrock of history. Without narratives, history would die as a discipline. Narratives tell us what happened, usually following the sequence of events as they happen, one event after the other—just as you might tell a story about something that happened to you this morning.

Good narrative history often looks easy to write because it is easy to read. In fact, storytelling is a complicated art. As in description, part of the art lies in a sense of what to include and what to exclude, what to believe and what to reject. Narrative must also take into account contradictions in the evidence and either resolve them or admit frankly that they cannot be resolved. Who fired the first shot on the morning of April 19, 1775, when British regular soldiers clashed with the minutemen on the Lexington Green in Massachusetts? The incident makes a nice subject for narrative history—but it is not an easy story to write. Sylvanus Wood, one of the minutemen, dictated his account of the battle over fifty years after he fought in it under the command of Captain John Parker. Here is part of what he said:

> Parker led those of us who were equipped to the north end of Lexington Common, near the Bedford Road, and formed us in single file. I was stationed about in the centre of the company. While we were standing, I left my place and went from one end of the company to the other and counted every man who was paraded, and the whole number was thirty-eight and no more. . . .
>
> The British troops approached us rapidly in platoons with a general officer on horseback at their head. The officer came up to within about two rods of the centre of the company, where I stood, the first platoon being about three rods distant. They were halted. The officer then

swung his sword, and said, "Lay down your arms, you damned rebels, or you are all dead men. Fire!" Some guns were fired by the British at us from the first platoon, but no person was killed or hurt, being probably charged only with powder.

Just at this time, Captain Parker ordered every man to take care of himself. The company immediately dispersed; and while the company was dispersing and leaping over the wall, the second platoon of the British fired and killed some of our men. There was not a gun fired by any of Captain Parker's company, within my knowledge.[5]

Paul Revere had been captured by the British in the middle of the night before the skirmish. He told the British that 500 men would be waiting for them in Lexington. Lieutenant John Barker of the British Army was with the British regiment called the King's Own. He wrote an account of the battle only a few days afterwards, and here is part of what he said:

About 5 miles on this side of a town called Lexington, which lay in our road, we heard there were some hundreds of people collected together intending to oppose us and stop our going on. At 5 o'clock we arrived there and saw a number of people, I believe between 2 and 300, formed in a common in the middle of the town. We still continued advancing, keeping prepared against an attack tho' without intending to attack them; but on our coming near them they fired one or two shots, upon which our men without any orders rushed in upon them, fired and put 'em to flight. Several of them were killed, we could not tell how many because they were got behind walls and into the woods. We had a man of the 10th Light Infantry wounded, nobody else hurt.[6]

How many American minutemen waited for the British on the green at Lexington that morning? The writer of a historical narrative must deal with the contradiction. You cannot pretend that the contradiction does not exist. Professor David Hackett Fischer, who has written the best book on the battles, did what you should do when

---

[5] Quoted in *The Spirit of Seventy-Six*, ed. Henry Steele Commager and Richard B. Morris (New York: Harper & Row, 1975), 82–83.

[6] Quoted in *The Spirit of Seventy-Six*, 70–71.

you face such a contradiction. He looked for more sources, and he discovered a number of other depositions given by members of the Lexington militia and eyewitnesses. These investigations allowed him to make a sensible deduction: Many of the men the British soldiers saw as they advanced on Lexington were spectators, and some other minutemen joined Parker and his band after Sylvanus Wood counted the group. Here is part of Fischer's absorbing narrative. We have left out his numerous footnotes; however, note his careful citation in the text of his sources:

> At the same moment the British officers were studying the militia on the Common in front of them. Paul Revere's warning of 500 men in arms echoed in their ears. As the officers peered through the dim gray light, the spectators to the right and left appeared to be militia too. Captain Parker's small handful of men multiplied in British eyes to hundreds of provincial soldiers. Pitcairn thought that he faced "near 200 of the rebels." Barker reckoned the number at "between two and three hundred."
>
> On the other side, the New England men also inflated the size of the Regular force, which was magnified by the length of its marching formation on the narrow road. As the militia studied the long files of red-coated soldiers, some reckoned the force at between 1200 and 1500 men. In fact there were only about 238 of all ranks in Pitcairn's six companies, plus the mounted men of Mitchell's patrol, and a few supernumeraries.
>
> The Lexington militia began to consult earnestly among themselves. Sylvanus Wood, a Woburn man who joined them, had made a quick count a few minutes earlier and found to his surprise that there were only thirty-eight militia in all. Others were falling into line, but altogether no more than sixty or seventy militia mustered on the Common, perhaps less. One turned to his captain and said, "There are so few of us it is folly to stand here."[7]

Fischer continues his absorbing story, working along the way to resolve the contradictions in his sources. By the time his readers get this far they have some understanding of why the British

---

[7] David Hackett Fischer, *Paul Revere's Ride* (New York and Oxford: Oxford University Press, 1994), 188–189.

overestimated the patriot force. In a detailed appendix, Fischer explains why he rejects Barker's number of "about 600" men in the British attacking force: Fischer went to the payroll rosters of the British army to see how many soldiers of the King's Own were collecting wages for their service. He recognized, as all historians must, that developing a narrative can be a complicated task. (After reading Fischer, we still think an argument may be made that Barker's number was correct, but that's another story.)

A good narrative begins by establishing some sort of tension, some kind of problem, that later development of the narrative should resolve. The beginning should arouse your curiosity. You read on to see how it comes out. Children's stories demonstrate the qualities of any good narrative: "Once upon a time a little girl named Cinderella lived in a house with her wicked stepmother and her two wicked stepsisters. Now the prince of the country gave a great ball, and he invited Cinderella's sisters, but poor Cinderella had to stay home and sweep out the ashes while her sisters went off to have a good time." You immediately know that Cinderella has troubles, that somehow the story is going to involve the sisters, the stepmother, the prince, and the ball. The story will reveal why all these details are introduced at the beginning.

A good narrative history has the same qualities. It is not merely a recitation of facts. It introduces elements in tension and the rest of the story dwells on resolving or explaining that tension. Do not introduce material into your essay at the beginning if you don't intend to do something with it later on.

A narrative should also have a climax that embodies the meaning the writer wants readers to take from the story. At the climax, everything comes together—the bill is passed, the battle is won or lost, the candidate is elected, the speech is made, the problem is solved or else explained. Because it gathers up all the threads and joins them to make the writer's point, the climax comes near the end of the paper. When you arrive at the climax, you are ready to wrap up your story, and your readers should feel that you have kept a promise made to them in the beginning. If you cannot think of a climax to your paper, you should reexamine your topic. If you cannot find a climactic point, you need to reorganize your story.

The story should move along, unburdened by unnecessary details. A good story can be enlivened by apt quotation, as in Fischer's narrative of the Battle of Lexington. But a principle of style worth remembering is that long block quotations frequently slow down a narrative, as does the inclusion of too many details. In telling a story, it is usually better to keep quotations short and pointed, and the examples limited, so that they clearly illustrate the events being recounted and readily lead to the conclusion you intend.

In the following narrative concerning the Battle of Adwa, fought in 1896 between Ethiopian forces of Emperor Menilek and Italian armies threatening to bring his country within Italy's northeastern African colonial orbit, Harold G. Marcus is spare in mentioning details and even more parsimonious in his use of quotation. He begins by indicating the plans of the Italian commander, General Oreste Baratieri, establishing an expectation of the outcome. Then he narrates the story of how the battle actually unfolded.

> The general and his army of 8,463 Italians and 10,749 Eritreans [local Africans] held the high ground between Adigrat and Idaga Hamus. Baratieri was prepared to outwit his enemy, whose limited supplies would have forced retirement southward, permitting Baratieri to claim victory and also advance deeper into Tigray. . . .
>
> At 9:00 P.M., on 28 February, the Italians began a forced march to the three hills that dominated the Ethiopian camp, to surprise and challenge Menilek's army. To secure his left Baratieri sent his reserve brigade to an unnamed, nearby fourth hill, but the Ethiopian guide, either through misdirection or sabotage, led the Italians astray. Not only was the left flank uncovered but also a quarter of the Italian force was rendered useless and vulnerable. So, even if Baratieri's army had occupied the high points and deployed in strong defensive positions on the frontal slopes, it was foredoomed to defeat. Indeed, the timing of the Italian attack, as a surprise on early Sunday morning, was all wrong.
>
> At 4:00 A.M., on 1 March, Menilek, [Empress] Taitou, and the rases [chief political and military subordinates of the Emperor] were at mass, which the Orthodox church celebrates early. It was a sad time,

since the food situation had forced the emperor to order camp to be struck on 2 March. His relief must have been great when a number of couriers and runners rushed in to report the enemy was approaching in force. The emperor ordered men to arms, and, as the soldiers lined up, priests passed before them hearing confession, granting absolution, and offering blessings. The green, orange, and red flags of Ethiopia were unfurled when the emperor appeared, and the soldiers cheered and cheered. At 5:30 A.M., Menilek's 100,000-man army moved forward, to confront an Italian force of 14,500 soldiers.

By 9:00 A.M., the outcome was obvious. The Italian center had crumbled, and other units were in danger of being flanked by Ethiopians who had found the gap in Baratieri's defenses. By noon, when retreat sounded, the Italians had paid dearly. Four thousand Europeans and 2,000 Eritreans had died, 1,428 of Baratieri's soldiers had been wounded, and 1,800 prisoners were held by the Ethiopians. All told, the Italian army lost 70 percent of its forces, a disaster for a modern army.

In sharp contrast, Menilek's forces suffered an estimated 4,000–7,000 killed and perhaps as many as 10,000 wounded, which made for an acceptably low loss ratio. The Italian enemy had been destroyed, whereas the Ethiopian army remained in being, strengthened by the weapons and matériel abandoned on the field. The victory was unequivocally Ethiopian.[8]

In telling the story of this imperial encounter, Marcus poses a problem and then narrates the story to its unexpected conclusion. Although there are many other sources available concerning the conflict at Adwa, including Italian official records, letters and diaries of soldiers, not to mention oral testimonies collected from some of the participants, Marcus wisely elects not to infuse his narrative with too much of this potentially extraneous information. He uses just enough evidence—primarily the numbers of soldiers engaged in the battle and the numbers of casualties—in a way that lends credibility to his account. And thus you are disposed to believe him when he goes on to conclude that Menilek's victory at the Battle of Adwa did "guarantee Ethiopia another generation and one-half of virtually

---

[8] Harold G. Marcus, *A History of Ethiopia* (Berkeley: University of California Press, 1994), 98–99.

unchallenged independence; it gave the country a status similar to that of Afghanistan, Persia, Japan, and Thailand as accepted anomalies in the imperialist world order."[9]

Of course, in your research you might just as well consult some of the numerous published (and perhaps, if your college or university has its own archive, also unpublished) collections of letters, as well as journals and collected papers. They offer similar opportunities for narrative writing about other stories concerning the past. Not just battles, but also the lives of individuals, and even the explanations they offer for the circumstances of their existence, can become fascinating subjects for your history papers. You could also construct a narrative based on one large source by extracting a story contained within it.

For example, the great Canadian explorer, Simon Fraser, kept a journal in 1808 as he looked for a navigable river passage he hoped would lead from central Canada to the Pacific Ocean. Had such a river existed, Canadians could have more easily transported furs from the Pacific coast to markets in the populous areas of Canada, and they might also have been able to lay claim to the territory that became the states of Washington and Oregon. Such a river did not exist. The river he found, ultimately named for him, runs into the Pacific considerably north of the Columbia River and the present border of Washington State, and it is not navigable through the mountains. His journal has been published, and it records his daring, his hopes, and his tribulations day by day.[10] Using it as a principal source, a great narrative may be constructed.

Whatever sources you use, be sure to pose these questions to yourself when you write historical narrative:

Writer's Checklist

_____ ✔ Why am I telling this story?
_____ ✔ What happened, and when did it begin and end?

---

[9] Marcus, *Ethiopia*, 100.

[10] Simon Fraser, *Letters and Journals, 1806–1808*, edited by W. Kaye Lamb (Toronto: Macmillan Canada, 1960).

_____ ✔ Who or what caused it to happen?
_____ ✔ Who were the major characters in the drama?
_____ ✔ What details must I tell, and what can I leave
out?
_____ ✔ What is the climax of the story?
_____ ✔ What does the story mean?

EXPOSITION

Expositions explain and analyze—philosophical ideas, causes of events, the significance of decisions, the motives of participants, the working of an organization, the ideology of a political party. Any time you set out to explain cause and effect, or the meaning of an event or an idea, you write in the expository mode.

As we have pointed out earlier in this chapter, exposition may coexist in an essay with other modes. The narrator who tells *what* happened usually devotes some paragraphs to telling *why* it happened—and so goes into expository writing. Some historical essays are fairly evenly balanced between narrative and exposition, telling both what happened and why, or else explaining the significance of the story. Many historical essays are primarily expositions, especially those that analyze and break down a text or event to tell readers what it means—even as they narrate what happened that makes the explanation necessary.

In college papers about history, exposition usually plays an important role. You may, for example, write an essay to answer this question: What did the founding fathers mean by the Second Amendment to the U.S. Constitution? That amendment reads, "A well-regulated militia, being necessary to the security of a free State, the right of the people to keep and bear arms, shall not be infringed." The essay you write in response would be an exposition. But it would probably include some narratives, perhaps the situation in 1789 when the Constitution was ratified, the situation today, or the decisions of courts in the past on cases brought under the Second Amendment.

The study of the influence of one thinker on another ("A comparison between Sir Thomas More's *Utopia* and Nicolo Machiavelli's *The Prince*"), or of one set of ideas on a historical process ("The view of human nature expressed in the *Federalist Papers*"), can make a good expository paper. You may even expound on the significance of some technological invention ("The Role of Steamboats in the European Colonization of Africa"). All of these subjects require analysis of texts, of events, or both. You must explain things, relate various texts to one another, make inferences, and perhaps ask some questions that no one can answer. When, in a speech in Quebec City in July 1967, Charles De Gaulle cried, "Vive Québec Libre," was he pursuing a policy? Or was he only trying once again to annoy the "Anglo-Saxons" whom he often treated with contempt because he thought they were contemptuous of France? It is hard to know. But the difficulty does not stop the historian from trying to answer the questions.

As an example, first consider this excerpt from one of the most famous books of the Renaissance, Baldessare Castiglione's *The Book of the Courtier*. Written for another time, you will see that it is not always easily understood by the contemporary reader.

There are also other exercises which, although not immediately dependent upon arms, still have much in common therewith and demand much manly vigor; and chief among these is the hunt, it seems to me because it has a certain resemblance to war. It is a true pastime for great lords, it befits a Courtier, and one understands why it was so much practiced among the ancients. He should also know how to swim, jump, run, throw stones; for besides their usefulness in war, it is frequently necessary to show one's prowess in such things, whereby a good name is to be won, especially with the crowd (with whom one must reckon after all). Another noble exercise and most suitable for a man at court is the game of tennis which shows off the disposition of body, the quickness and litheness of every member, and all the qualities that are brought out by almost every other exercise. Nor do I deem vaulting on horseback to be less worthy, which, though it is tiring and difficult, serves more than anything else to make a man agile and dexterous; and besides its usefulness, if such agility is accompanied by grace, in my opinion it makes a finer show than any other. If, then, our Courtier is more than fairly expert in such exercises, I think he ought to put aside all others, such as vaulting on the ground, rope-walking, and the like, which smack of the juggler's trade and little befit a gentleman.[11]

Now, consider the following exposition that uses this passage as part of a general treatment of the Renaissance. Insofar as is possible, the writer of this exposition puts the thoughts of Castiglione into other words that may be more familiar and, hence, more understandable for readers today.

> Baldessare Castiglione's *The Book of the Courtier*, the most frequently translated and printed book of the sixteenth century other than the Bible, presents itself as a dialogue on the qualities that make a good courtier. Courtiers, as the name implies, were members of a prince's court or entourage, helping him in various ways to rule his domain. In the sixteenth century, when Italy was divided among multitudes of city-states, princes needed talented men to help conduct finances, war, diplomacy, and other affairs. Without such servants and counselors, princes might lose power over a populace that was often fickle and rebellious.
>
> Courtiers rose on their talents but also on their ability to get along with other people and impress their princes—not unlike the way people rise today in the corporate and political worlds. Castiglione's dialogue became not only an entertainment but also a handbook. Aspiring courtiers read it to learn how to conduct themselves as gentlemen and how to rise. It was the

---

[11] Baldessare Castiglione, *The Book of the Courtier*, trans. Charles S. Singleton (Garden City, NY: Doubleday, 1959), 38–39.

manners book of its day, popular alike with Spanish kings and English puritans.

Castiglione throughout writes on two levels. On one level, the courtiers in his dialogue discuss ways of becoming more useful, better men. It is good to hunt, for example, for hunting calls for many of the same skills required in war. Evidently he refers to life in the open air, to riding on horseback in the chase, and to marksmanship—all helpful training for soldiers. Swimming, jumping, running, and throwing stones offer what we would call physical conditioning and provide basic training for war.

On another level, Castiglione's characters are always concerned not only to better their skills but also to make a good impression. By performing feats of physical strength and agility, one wins a good name with the crowd "with whom one must reckon after all." Tennis, with its leaping and quickness, displays the body. Jumping on horseback both helps a man become "agile and dexterous" and "makes a finer show than any other." Some things make a bad show and are to be avoided no matter how useful they may be as bodily exercises. For some reason Castiglione cites "vaulting on the ground" as an act to be avoided, perhaps because that sort of leaping was a game of peasants who could not afford jumping horses. "Rope-walking," balancing oneself on a tight rope, is also scorned because it is one of the tricks of "jugglers," the traveling entertainers who put on shows for city crowds much as their spiritual descendants do today. Such entertainers were considered lower class and even slightly dishonorable.

Throughout his book, these two qualities come to the fore again and again—skill and reputation. The good courtier in Castiglione's mind possessed both. Thousands of readers pored over his pages to learn not only what they should be but also what they should seem not to be.

This exposition tries to make sense of a text from the past. The world has greatly changed from Castiglione's times—although some things remain similar. The exposition explains his ideas, defines terms, and provides a context for his thoughts. Castiglione used the common word *juggler*, which you might take to mean someone who tosses several balls in the air at once and catches them without dropping any of them. The older meaning of the term in both Castiglione's Italian and sixteenth-century English was a street entertainer, usually some sort of magician. By explaining this broader use of the term, the writer makes the expounded text more clear. Always define the essential terms of your exposition.

This exposition also includes some inferences. The writer infers that juggling is forbidden to the courtier because it smacks of deceit, and courtiers are supposed to be honest. The writer infers that jumping or "vaulting" on the ground is forbidden because that sort of athletic activity is common to peasants who cannot afford horses. Peasants in Europe at this time were scorned by the educated classes who might be courtiers and who might read Castiglione's book. One cannot prove an inference, but inferences provide plausible explanations that may help fill out the meaning of a text. These inferences show a writer trying to make sense of things, and readers appreciate such thinking as long as it is credible and stays within the boundaries of the plausible.

When you decide to write an exposition on a particular subject in one of your essays, be sure to reflect on these questions:

Writer's Checklist

- _____ ✔ Is this explanation really necessary?
- _____ ✔ Have I provided a context for this analysis?
- _____ ✔ Do I define the essential terms?
- _____ ✔ Have I clearly identified the crucial causes and/or significance?
- _____ ✔ Are my inferences credible and plausible?
- _____ ✔ Have I clarified the meaning of what I am explaining?

ARGUMENT

Historians and others use argument in their writing to take a position on a controversial subject. As we have suggested at the start of this chapter, it can be said that every essay contains an argument in that every essay is built around a proposition that the writer wants us to believe. Yet in common usage, an argument is part of a debate, a dialogue between opposing views—sometimes many opposing views. Arguments include exposition, for they must explain the writer's point of view. An argument also seeks to prove that other points of view are wrong.

Arguments are most interesting when the issues are important and when all sides are fair to each other. The questions that create good arguments arise naturally as historians do research, weigh evidence, and make judgments that may not persuade others. Was Christianity, as Edward Gibbon held in the eighteenth century, a major cause for the decline and fall of the Roman Empire? Was Martin Luther a failure or a success? Did Al Smith lose the presidential election of 1928 to Herbert Hoover because Smith was a Catholic? Was slavery the main cause of the American Civil War? Have the poor of Cuba been better or worse off under the communist dictatorship of Fidel Castro than they were under Fulgencia Batista, the dictator Castro replaced?

The writing of history abounds with arguments about what happened and why. They arise because the evidence can be interpreted in different ways according to the assumptions of the historians themselves. Sometimes arguments continue until a consensus is gradually achieved. Did the German General Staff expect England to fight for Belgian neutrality if Germany invaded Belgium in 1914? For a long time many historians claimed that if England had declared itself clearly before fighting started, Germany would not have sent armies into Belgium—thereby thrusting the world into war. But since the work of German historian Fritz Fischer, most historians have come around to the view that Germany planned all along to fight the English. Sometimes arguments rage for years, die down, smolder awhile, and flame up again. Did President Harry S. Truman drop atom bombs on Japan because he feared that an invasion of the Japanese home islands by American troops would result in a million American casualties? Or did he know that the Japanese were already defeated and eager to surrender, and did he drop the bombs because he wanted to demonstrate the weapon to the dangerous Russians who, he recognized, would be the major foes to the United States after the war? The controversy over these questions raged for a time in the 1960s, died down, and has risen again in the past decade.

In any important historical issue, you will find disagreement among historians. The disagreements are valuable in that they discourage becoming frozen in an intolerance of opposition, and debates may actually encourage toleration in the present. The disagreements also help readers see the sources in a different light. Disagreements thrive in book reviews. A historian who disagrees with another will make a counterargument to a book the reviewer thinks is incorrect. Jacob Burckhardt's *History of the Renaissance in Italy,* published in 1860, has provoked a virtual library of response: reviews, articles, and even books arguing that he was right or wrong in his interpretation of the Renaissance—or arguing that he was partly right and partly wrong. Frederick Jackson Turner's frontier thesis concerning United States history has been similarly provocative.

The usual experience of the student of history is to study a great deal and to become convinced that someone else's argument is wrong, or at least off the mark. Francis Russell's books on the Sacco and Vanzetti case represent this kind of discovery. The popular consensus among modern American historians was that Sacco and Vanzetti were innocent Italian immigrants hounded to their deaths by a vicious Yankee society for murders they did not commit. In 1955 Russell wrote an article supporting this point of view, published first in the *Antioch Review* and reprinted three years later with photographs in *American Heritage.* But as Russell continued to ponder the case, he slowly changed his mind. His publication of *Tragedy in Dedham* and *Sacco and Vanzetti: The Case Resolved* represents a crushing attack on the previous consensus.

Stay tuned to your own thoughts when you read sources. Where do arguments seem weak? Where do you feel uneasy about your own arguments? Can you see another conclusion in the evidence? Often good argument is a matter of common sense: Can you believe that something might have happened the way a writer tells you it happened? Many people who hated Franklin D. Roosevelt argued that he knew about the Japanese attack on Pearl Harbor in 1941 before it happened but kept it secret because he wanted the United States to go to war. Such a conspiracy would have involved dozens if not thousands of people—those who had broken the Japanese secret code for sending messages to the military and diplomats, those who monitored Japanese broadcasts, those who translated them and took the translations to the White House and the State Department, and the officials to whom all of them reported. Is it plausible that such a vast conspiracy could have taken place without anyone ever stepping forward to talk about it, especially since any such report could have earned millions of dollars in book contracts? Experience with human beings and their apparently uncontrollable yearning to tell secrets would seem to indicate that the answer to such a question would be no.

Good arguments, though, are founded on skepticism. Come to history as a doubter. Study the evidence over and over. Read what other historians have said. See what the sources say. Listen to your own uneasiness. Do not take anything for granted. And when you decide to argue, be as careful—and as civil—as possible. To help in this process, here are some suggestions for making convincing arguments. Study them carefully and keep them in mind as you write and when you read the arguments of others.

1. Always state your argument quickly and concisely, as early as possible in your paper.

Get to the point in your first paragraph if possible. You will help yourself in making an argument if you state your premises early, shortly after telling us what your argument is going to be. *Premises* are assumptions on which your arguments are based. In writing about history, you may assume that some sources are reliable and some are not, and you will base your argument accordingly. You must then explain why you think one source is more reliable than another. Having done so, you can move towards your argument based on the premise of reliability.

All arguments are based on premises. Most Western historians take it for granted that Japanese militarism as it developed in the 1930s was disastrous for Japan and the world. But Japanese historians may assume that such militarism was the last effort to preserve a traditional society that had endured for a very long time. That society emphasized collective rather than individual values, and the effort of the Japanese military could be seen as an unsuccessful but valiant effort to preserve the good of the past against Western imperialism. No matter how objectionable such a position may seem to you, given the millions of deaths caused in Asia by Japanese aggression, the position makes you look at things in a different light, perhaps allowing you to see just how aggressive Britain, the United States, and other Western powers seemed to the Japanese at the time.

2. When you make an assertion essential to your case, provide some examples as evidence.

Journalists almost always follow this principle. A general statement is followed by a quotation or some other concrete reference to the evidence that provides support for the assertion. Readers need some reason to believe you. In writing about volunteer nursing by French women during World War I, historian Margaret H. Darrow deals with a paradox. The myths of war held that it was "full of honor, courage, heroism, self-sacrifice, and manliness." Nurses treating the wounded and the dying were caught not only by the power of the myth but also by the reality of what they saw; they had a hard time reconciling the two. Darrow offers this observation on the problem:

> Few memoirs resolved the tension between the rhetoric of noble suffering and heroic sacrifice and the reality of dirt, pain, fear, and fatigue,

with most memoirs swinging from one mode to the other without any attempt at reconciliation. For example, Noëlle Roger began her description of a ward of seriously wounded soldiers with the claim that "each of these men had lived a glorious adventure." She then depicted the shrieking pain of a man brought from the operating table, the rigid terror of a tetanus victim, and the hallucinations of a shell-shock case. However, her intent was not irony; she did not seem to notice—or could not express—that none of these were glorious adventures.[12]

Here is a standard pattern in historical writing—follow it whenever you can. The writer makes a general statement: "Few memoirs resolved the tensions between the rhetoric of noble suffering and heroic sacrifice and the reality of dirt, pain, fear, and fatigue, with most memoirs swinging from one mode to the other without any attempt at reconciliation." Then she offers a quotation and a summary of the evidence. A reader will be inclined to believe the general statement because the author has provided specific evidence for it.

3. Always give the fairest possible treatment to those against whom you may be arguing.

Never distort the work of someone who disagrees with your position. Such distortions are cowardly and unfair, and if you are found out, readers will reject you and your work, the good part along with the bad. Treat your adversaries as erring friends, not as foes to be slain, and you will always be more convincing to the great mass of readers who want writers to be fair and benign in argument. The most effective scholarly arguments are carried on courteously and without bitterness or anger. When you argue, remember the admonition of the Prophet Isaiah: "In quietness and confidence shall be your strength."

---

[12] Margaret H. Darrow, "French Volunteer Nursing and the Myth of War Experience in World War I," *American Historical Review*, 101(1996):100.

4. Always admit weakness in your argument and acknowledge those facts that opponents might raise against your position.

If you deny obvious truths about the subject of your argument, knowledgeable readers will see what you are doing and will lose confidence in your sense of fairness. Most arguments have a weak point somewhere. Otherwise, there would be no argument. If you admit the places where your argument is weak and consider counterarguments fairly, giving your reasons for rejecting them, you will build confidence in your judgments among readers.

Concession is vital in argument. You may concede that some evidence stands against your proposition. But you may then argue either that the evidence is not as important or as trustworthy as the evidence you adduce for your point of view. Or you may argue that the contrary evidence has been misinterpreted. In either case, you acknowledge that you know about the contrary facts, and you rob your foes of seeming to catch you in ignorance.

5. Stay on the subject throughout your essay so your argument is not submerged in meaningless detail.

Inexperienced writers sometimes try to throw everything they know into an essay as if it were a soup, and the more ingredients the better. They have worked hard to gather the information. They find their sources interesting. They want readers to see how much work they have done, how much they know. So they pad papers with much information irrelevant to the topic at hand. Sometimes they begin with pages and pages of background information and get into their argument only after they have bewildered readers with a story that does not need to be told. Get to your point. Trust your readers. Moreover, trust yourself. Make your arguments economical. Do as much as you can in as few words as possible.

As you follow these suggestions for writing an essay espousing your point of view on a historical subject, here are some questions to ask yourself about an argument you have advanced:

Writer's Checklist

_____   ✔ Is this subject worth arguing about?

_____   ✔ Have I gathered enough evidence to make an argument?

_____   ✔ Do I represent the views of my opponents in a way they would consider fair?

_____   ✔ Have I developed my argument logically?

_____   ✔ Is my use of evidence accurate and related to my argument?

_____   ✔ Have I tried to prove too much?

Thinking about modes of writing will help you define more precisely the reason for your paper in history. Too frequently in history courses, students start writing without having any idea of the point they finally want to make about a topic. The instructor says, "Write a ten-page paper," and the student thinks only, "I must fill up ten pages." Well, you can fill up ten pages by copying the telephone book, but that won't be a good paper in a history course! Thinking about the modes will clarify your writing task. It will also help your readers understand your purposes quickly. When we immediately understand what a writer is doing in a paper, our grade thermometer rises dramatically, and we become prepared to dispense high marks. Most instructors of our experience feel the same way. One of the hardest tasks an instructor faces is to have to read four or five pages into a paper before beginning to understand what the topic is. Help your hardworking instructor—and thereby help yourself—by writing papers in which your command of the modes of writing will make your purposes clear.

GATHERING INFORMATION

■ ■ ■

All writing is hard work if it is done well. Writing history has special problems; we have already discussed many of them in this book. It is sometimes easy to assume that simply being familiar with life—or some particular aspect of human interactions—is sufficient. George F. Kennan, the American diplomat and historian, confessed to making this assumption when he accepted the 1957 National Book Award for his *Russia Leaves the War*:

> I am afraid that I took up the historian's task somewhat casually, never doubting that it would be easier to tell about diplomacy than to conduct it—and not nearly so great a responsibility. But as this work gradually wrought its discipline upon me, I was both surprised and sobered to realize not only how difficult but also how important it was.[1]

Few people will be as honored for writing history as Kennan, but most of you can learn to do it successfully—and thereby learn to do other writing well, too. The problems of gathering evidence, analyzing it, organizing it, and presenting it in a readable form are part of many writing tasks in the world of business, government, and the professions that include law, engineering, and others. So you should expect to use your skills developed in writing history papers in whatever your future career may be.

---

[1] Quoted in *The National Book Award: Writers on Their Craft and Their World* (New York: Book-of-the-Month Club, 1990), 18.

All writers use some sort of process—a series of steps that lead them from discovering a subject to writing a final draft. Different writers work according to different rituals. The two of us developed somewhat different ways of approaching our own writing. And we certainly recognize that in the decade or so since this *Short Guide* first appeared, changes in the academic world—most especially in the areas of electronic technologies—have brought about changes in our writing habits. Many of those changes have made aspects of the work somewhat easier. But we also believe these changes have, as well, made some writing tasks more difficult. Overall, we remain convinced that good writing is hard work and, above all, requires patience and practice.

Eventually you will find your own way of doing things. In this chapter and the next, we shall walk you through some common stages of the work that history writers must undertake on their way to creating books or essays. At the outset, though, we want to make clear this is seldom a linear process—one step following categorically after another—leading directly to a written product. One step may instead take you back to reexamine what you have previously done; only then will you be able to finish the task at hand. Even after you have gathered, analyzed, and organized your information, writing the complete essay will likely take you back to those steps as well. The following suggestions may help you by showing how others write, but in the end you must develop the writing process that suits you best.

FINDING A TOPIC

History papers begin with an assignment, usually expressed in the syllabus the instructor passes out at the beginning of the course. Read that assignment with great care. You will find in it the kind of topic your instructor wants you to write about, the evidence he or she wants you to use, and the length the paper should be. Follow those instructions carefully. The topic may be general within the limits of the course: "You will write a ten-page paper on a topic agreed on by you and the instructor." Or the topic may be explicit: "Write a ten-page paper on the reasons for the appeal of Lenin's 'April Theses' in 1917 during the Russian Revolution." In some courses you may be required to write a more historiographical paper: "Alfred Crosby, Daniel Headrick, and Edward Said have all written books about imperialism. Write a ten-page paper exploring the differences in their attitudes towards modern imperialism."

But many assignments in history courses are general, and for most students finding a topic in such circumstances is an ordeal. Professional historians frequently have the same problem, so don't be discouraged in your search. The ability to find your own topic reflects both how well you know the material and how you think about it. Defining your own topic is good discipline. A liberal arts education—including education in history—should teach you to ask questions and ponder meanings in every text and topic you encounter in life. And, as we have suggested, it is an essential part of historical writing that you do so.

Start with your own interests. You should be curious about people, events, documents, or problems considered in your courses. This curiosity should cause you to pose some questions naturally, and especially about topics related in some way to what you are studying. For example, in one course you might study the Russian Revolution of 1917, in another American obsession with the dangers of Communism and the Soviet Union during the cold war, while in a third you might consider the music of Sergey Prokofiev. In studying and reading about any of these subjects, your curiosity might well lead you to thinking about the half-century history of the Soviet Union and its collapse in just a matter of months, something unforeseen (if sometimes hoped for!) by very few responsible persons. That amazing event should stimulate multitudes of questions you might ask to satisfy your curiosity about how such a thing could happen. And any number of those questions could easily help you find an excellent topic for a history paper.

As you read and attend class, you can help yourself by keeping notes in which you not only jot down what you learn, but also the questions that occur to you, including—and perhaps especially—those without obvious answers. Keep a systematic record of those questions, perhaps in a separate section of your class notebook. Or you might even keep a small, separate notebook—or a special computer file—entirely for these ideas and questions; a collection of such questions will have lots of potential paper topics in it.

And never be afraid to consider a well-worn topic. Why did the Confederate army under Robert E. Lee lose at Gettysburg? What qualities of Christianity made it attractive to people in the Roman Empire during the first three centuries after Christ? What was humanism in the Renaissance? At first glance you may think that everything has been said that can be said. Indeed, many things have been written on all these topics. But when you look at the sources, you may discover that you have an insight that is new and different and worth exploring. That possibility is especially good if you study a few documents carefully and use them as windows that open onto the age or the event that produced them.

Sometimes you can find interesting topics in history by staying attuned to your own interests and experiences. If you are a religious person, you may naturally try to understand religious influences in the past. Do not use a history paper to convert someone to your own religious point of view. But religion is one of the most important continuing forces in world affairs, and it sometimes strikes us as odd that students do not think to apply their religious interest to exploring how religion has influenced historical events. The same is true of interests such as sports, food, fashion, and other elements of life. We have both sometimes wondered when the French love affair with dogs began and what historical significance it may have. History is a much more open discipline than it once was, and with a little searching you may be able to translate one of your own consuming interests or particular personal circumstances into a good research paper. One of our students wondered how she might answer questions from her children about the bananas they frequently ate for breakfast. So she did some reading, thought about the problem, and posed a number of questions; the final result was an excellent history essay on how bananas became such a popular food in our country even though almost none are actually grown commercially here.

We must, however, repeat an important axiom: Yours must be an *informed* interest. You have to know something before you write anything about history. Do not write an opinionated essay merely off the top of your head; your argument needs to be more than a restatement of your prejudices. Good historians read, ask questions of their reading, read again, and try to get things right. They try to think through their initial questions, examining the many facets of the problem and focusing on a narrower topic, one manageable within the limits of the essay they expect to write.

LIMITING YOUR TOPIC

Considering the application of informed interest brings us to some essential wisdom that every writer must learn. We have mentioned it already, but it needs to be repeated. In our experience the most common flaw in student papers is that the topics are so broad that the essays have no focus and cannot therefore develop an original idea based on the evidence. You cannot write an interesting and original paper entitled "Woodrow Wilson" or "Mackenzie King" or "Susan B. Anthony." In 2000 or even 6000 words, you can only do a summary of a person's life—suitable perhaps for an encyclopedia but not for a thoughtful essay that tries to argue a special point. Very similar difficulties would apply should you decide to write on "The Causes of World War II," or even "The Reasons for the Renaissance"; both topics are so broad as to defy any meaningful analysis in an essay of ten pages or so. Pick a limited issue with available texts or other evidence that you can study in depth and write about within the assigned space.

Even if your instructor assigns a specific topic as the basis of your essay, it is almost always appropriate to limit, or at least focus, the topic further. Consider the topic we mentioned above: "Alfred

Crosby, Daniel Headrick, and Edward Said have all written books about imperialism. Write a ten-page paper exploring the differences in their attitudes towards modern imperialism." You will, of course, need to read the books of the three authors and determine the thesis each presents. Then you will need to compare the three views, analyzing how they are similar and different. These comparisons should lead you to a conclusion, and with it a specific argument for your essay "exploring the differences" in their theories about the causes and consequences of imperialism.

Whatever your writing assignment, or the general topic you first identify, there are usually ways to limit your topic either by narrowing its scope or adjusting your angle of vision. The scope of a broad topic such as imperialism, for example, might be reduced by focusing on the colonial ambitions of a single country. Even the scope of French imperialism could be further limited by considering French imperialism in the Caribbean, or even the island of Martinique alone. The geographic scope of your topic can frequently be reduced by also considering elements of time. You might consider limiting your consideration of imperialism to the period before—or after—the Napoleanic wars, for example. Or you might wish to consider the impact of twentieth-century developments—such as the League of Nations or the United Nations—on French imperialism in the western hemisphere.

But in addition to limiting the scope of your topic, you might also consider changing your angle of vision. As we have previously noted, historians in this new century have successfully explored a much broader range of questions about the past. In this environment you have many more choices about how to refocus your topic. Years ago the usual concerns regarding colonialism were of grand politics or perhaps the details of colonial administration. You might also find occasional biographies of the key leaders. But with the changes taking place in the way historians observe the past, there are many more angles you might pursue to narrow the topic.

You might ask questions not just about individuals, but about groups of people. How did French imperialism impact the various social classes in France itself? Or what were the effects of French imperial practice on the indigenous inhabitants of Martinique? Did French education policies in its Caribbean colonies increase the educational level of women as well as men? Why was the regulation of sexuality a significant part of French imperial policy? There are many other such questions which might well occur to you. In short, allow your curiosity to open new avenues of questioning as you consider your topic. Surely you will find several ways you might further narrow that topic so that you can craft an interesting essay with a new argument.

In the process of making your essay more focused, however, you also need to keep in mind that your topic must be defined according to the sources available. In some cases your assignment will do this for you. But, more often, you will need to determine what sources you might consult. We find it sad when students take this advice as a signal to limit their search for information. Instead we encourage them to search more widely and find whatever sources they can. And in the academic environment at the start of this new century, there are almost always more sources available than you would imagine. Thus your challenge in narrowing the topic should be to simultaneously expand your quest for usable information.

Considering Potential Sources

There was a time when our sole advice to students seeking potential sources for their essays was to go to the library. Of course that has become much too limiting an approach as the field of "library science" has been growing to become "information science." Yet we believe that advice of the earlier editions of this book is still appropriate: Smart students and smart professors should learn to talk to reference librarians about sources of information. And it transcends matters of books and encyclopedias to encompass electronic search techniques and information retrieval.

Several years ago when one of us was engaged in research about American westward expansion in the 1850s, a reference librarian at the University of Tennessee supplied the answer to a question: How might someone have amputated an injured arm on the Western plains at that time? In a wink she produced a little book called *Gunn's Domestic Medicine* published in 1831. It provided complete and optimistic instructions which, as it turned out, found their way into a historical novel wherein one of the characters followed those very directions. Several doctors, on reading that account, have expressed cautious astonishment that a historian and mere writer knew so much about amputating arms. Perhaps the author flunked out of medical school? No, simply credit a good reference librarian!

Of course, putting the information from the source to use was the writer's achievement. But that was made possible by the intervention, in this case directly, by a person who pointed the writer to a potential source. It is up to you to seek out such resources and to ask for assistance when you need it. However, if you were to ask a reference librarian every single question that occurred to you about your topic, it is unlikely the results would be nearly so satisfactory.

The advent of reliable electronic communications has made it possible for you also to seek help from any number of historians and other scholars. Discussion groups of all sorts roar across the Internet every moment, and anyone with an interest in a particular subject or area can join most of these at no charge. Many are in reality electronic bull sessions where people chat in real time about Shakespeare or historical subjects or heaven knows what. Now and then something valuable gets said. Of more interest to research historians are somewhat more formal discussion lists comprised of people interested in a particular topic to which the list is dedicated.

Some discussion lists, however, remain free-for-all forums where anything sent to the list is immediately resent to all of the e-mailboxes in the group. Others are presided over by one or more moderators or editors who ensure only messages germane to the list topic will be posted. Many in the latter group are of interest to historians, especially those sponsored by the scholarly collective known as H-Net, Humanities and Social Sciences Online. You can find the directory of more than one hundred H-Net discussion networks at

<http://www.h-net.msu.edu>. These offer the opportunity to ask questions about many subjects—books and articles, puzzles in evidence, current problems—anything at all relating to the interests the group is intended to serve. Each has its own rules, including ways to join and ways to cut off your subscription. We would offer one note of caution: a danger of belonging to several such groups is that your mailbox quickly fills up, and you get a lot of information you don't want or need. Still, such groups do form valuable scholarly communities, and you can tap into them in various ways not merely to ask your own questions but also to eavesdrop on postings that may aid you in your research.

You may also have opportunities to contact historians directly. When you read a book or article by a living historian, you may be able to reach that person by e-mail with a question and often receive in return a generous reply. The American Historical Association publishes an annual directory of Departments of History that includes a list of individual historians with e-mail addresses for many of them. Still others have e-mail addresses listed on the World Wide Web pages of the universities where they are employed. Both of us have received numerous inquiries directly from students and through discussion networks to which we belong, and we have tried to respond whenever we can be of help.

But to obtain such help, either directly or through some form of discussion network, it is always to your advantage to have located some information prior to making your inquiries. Your questions will take on greater seriousness if you have already made some effort to find at least a few of the basic materials that seem relevant to your topic. There are a variety of means you should use to begin seeking potential sources. Increasingly these are found in various electronic formats, while others are still available in more traditional print forms. You should become familiar with such resources available in both electronic and print versions.

Read encyclopedia articles and other reference books to get a broad overview of the topic. If you look up the same subject in many different reference works, many essential facts about your topic will be stamped in your memory. And don't forget that old reference books are valuable for providing widely held beliefs about topics when those books were published. Your library reference room will have standard general encyclopedias—the multivolume sets such as *Britannica, Americana,* and *Collier's,* and single-volume encyclopedias such as *The New Columbia Encyclopedia* (one of our favorites). Many encyclopedias are also available in electronic formats; frequently one of them may be included with a software package sold with new computers. Some others may also be available through the electronic networks in your library.

Look also into reference materials that may be specifically addressed to your field of inquiry. You will find any number of subjects considered in reference works available on the World Wide Web. And there will be many specialized topics treated in encyclopedias, dictionaries, and other reference books available in your library. Not only broad fields of study, such as art or music, but also historical specialties such as colonialism or even the history of peace and peacemaking are considered in valuable reference volumes. One we consult often is the five-volume *Dictionary of the History of Ideas* in which you may often find information about ideas you intend to discuss in your history essay. If you choose a topic related to religion, you might consult *The New Catholic Encyclopedia* in fifteen volumes that contain a treasury of information on religious figures and religious movements of all sorts. *The New Standard Jewish Encyclopedia* provides a similar source for the history of the Jewish people and Judaism.

If your topic involves prominent individuals, you should consult one of the many biographical directories created for both broad and more narrow subjects of study. The *Dictionary of National Biography* is indispensable for any work on British history. *The Dictionary of American Biography* is inferior and sometimes disappointing, but there one can find interesting information about important Americans who may be subjects of historical research. Many libraries have old nineteenth-century biographical encyclopedias, and these are not to be scorned although the articles are nearly always laudatory, and it seems as if the people—nearly all of them men—paid in some way to have their names included, perhaps by buying the books.

Do not hesitate to use reference works in foreign languages. Even if you don't read the language or don't read it well, you may locate illustrations or maps or other useful materials. If you have had a year or two of study in the language, you may discover that you can read the articles far better than you suspected. That discovery may draw you into further use of it, an advantage to any student of history and essential to advanced work in most historical fields. Some of the articles you find—as is true of many reference works in English—will have brief bibliographies at the end listing standard works where you can find more detailed information on a subject.

Among the most important reference resources for historians are bibliographies on a huge variety of topics, some compiled by scholars specifically as reference works and others included by historians in their books and articles. Often you will find numerous bibliographies in library reference collections, and you may frequently locate others using library catalogues by looking for or adding the subcategory "bibliography" to the subjects you are searching for. There are a number of valuable general bibliographies as well. Be sure, for example, you consult the widely available *American Historical Association Guide to Historical Literature*, third edition, edited by Mary Beth Norton and Pamela Gerardi (New York, Oxford University Press, 1995). These two large and heavy volumes are a rich mine of information about books and articles on every aspect of history throughout the world. You may also find some bibliographic references on the World Wide Web; we will have more to say on that subject shortly. A few bibliographies are annotated. That is, the compiler offers a brief comment on the books, articles and other materials cited. It is possible that the writer may judge some sources too harshly, some too generously. But such a bibliography usually provides worthwhile information about the contents of books and articles.

Always compile your own bibliography from the start of your research, even when you are merely looking for potential sources.

By starting early you will save yourself much grief. All too often students have come to us as they are completing the final version of a history essay asking for additional bibliographic information, including—on more than one occasion—the title of "that little green book" on their topic. You should keep a systematic record of the full bibliographic references to books, articles, and other sources you locate as well as to recommendations for further reading in the bibliographies appended to these sources. You may wish to jot down the information in a notebook or on small index cards. The value of cards—that they may be easily reorganized or added to as the numbers of your references grow—has been superseded by the capacity to do the same using a word-processing program on a computer. Keeping your project's bibliography in a word processing file will also make it easier to keep backup copies just in case something dreadful might happen to destroy all your efforts. Remember, though, the hazards of fire and theft (as well as other threats) respect neither electronic disks nor paper note cards.

In addition to the bibliographies prepared by scholars, you also need to consult a variety of indexing materials to build your own list of potential sources. Among the most valuable are indexes that will help you locate articles in magazines and scholarly journals. Most of these have their origins in the venerable *Readers Guide to Periodical Literature*, which has been regularly published since 1900. Updates appear throughout the year, and at the end of each year a large, comprehensive edition is published. The *Reader's Guide* surveys only magazines intended for a general audience. Do not scorn this purpose. Although you will not find articles published in the specialized journals intended for professional historians, you may find interesting, well written articles by important specialists when consulting the *Reader's Guide*.

In recent decades other indexes have appeared to aid researchers in the humanities, social sciences, and many other fields of study in building their bibliographies. Originally published in monthly or yearly volumes, the *Reader's Guide* and similar indexes required writers to pore through many separate volumes to find information on their topics, searching under key words or categories assigned by human indexers to the articles in a wide variety of publications. Yet the time spent in searching through such materials— and also learning to master the sometimes cryptic notation used to provide the information—almost always was rewarded by the discovery of potential source material.

More recently, many such indexes have moved to electronic formats. This has been a boon to writers, as often a single search using a well chosen keyword, may yield a large number of entries for scrutiny. It is likely your library has arranged for your access to several such databases either through CD-ROM storage or via secure connections to and/or links from its own Web page. Few of those electronic indexes have yet to include more than just a few years of index results, so you will want to ascertain the time limitations of a particular electronic index and then consult the bound volumes of previous years, if they are available. Only then can you be confident that you have made a thorough search for potential information.

In a few cases these electronic databases may also permit you to locate the text of entire articles, and many others have thoughtful abstracts actually prepared by expert readers. Often using such abstracts can save you time, but you should be cautious in assuming they will always provide clear and complete indications of an article's content. Two particularly important indexes for historians are *Historical Abstracts* and *America: History and Life*. Particularly strong in its coverage of world and European subjects, *Historical Abstracts* has appeared each year for many decades and in electronic formats since 1981. Its pages, disks, and now World Wide Web files contain thousands of abstracts of books and articles indexed according to author, subject, period, and place. You can browse the abstracts for materials related to almost any historical topic. *America: History and Life*, updated annually, includes article abstracts and citations focusing on American history, including an index to book reviews. It goes back to 1964 and, like *Historical Abstracts*, is a fabulous resource. Both of these are widely available in most college and university libraries; you should consult with a reference librarian about how to access them in your library. It may be that you will need to consult the bound volumes for some earlier years of these indexes and perhaps for all of the years when using other indexes.

Of course you should also make use of the catalog in your local library. In many ways this is one of your best guides to material on your topic, even though it is usually limited to the books and other media actually available to you in that particular library. In some ways that is an advantage, as those materials have been specifically selected for inclusion in the collections. You can therefore have some assurance that they have been included not on a whim but with a particular purpose in mind. So if you have not already done so, early in your quest for material on your topic, you will want to learn how to use your local library catalog.

Although there are a variety of systems in use by libraries to present their catalogs for use, most have similar features. Online catalogs usually allow you to search for materials by *author* and *title* as well as by *subject* or *keyword*. Keep in mind that for a library catalog, the subject usually refers to a uniform set of subject headings created by the Library of Congress. You will have to enter these exactly for a subject search to be successful. Your library may have a collection of bound volumes containing all these subject headings, listed alphabetically. But it will likely be easier to choose the *long* or *full* catalog record of a work you have already identified to see what some appropriate subject headings for your topic may be. Easier still, you can search most library catalogs by *keyword*, usually a name or topic of particular interest to you. And most often you can also refine that search by either including or excluding other particular terms or specifying that a particular phrase should appear exactly as you have given it. Most catalogs have easy links to instructions to help you make such advanced searches. The results, however, will only be to materials which have been preselected for inclusion in your library. Do not limit your initial search for material to just what is easily at hand.

In the early stages of your quest, you will want to discover as many potential sources as possible. One resource only available recently is an integrated online catalog of almost twelve million bibliographic records from the Library of Congress; you can access it at <http://catalog.loc.gov>. As in most online catalogs, you can search by *title*, *subject*, and *keyword*. But its *name* search feature—rather than simply identifying authors of books—will also take you to other information on particular people of interest to you. Often this extensive catalog will help you locate information about earlier editions of particular books or additional works by historians and other writers of special interest for your topic. The time you spend looking at this resource and studying its online directions and user assistance pages will surely be rewarded, sometimes with many more materials than you imagined existed!

Indeed, that may also be the result of your attempts to find information using the vast and still-growing potential of the World Wide Web. We have already suggested several ways to use this resource. We certainly recognize the entire Internet is now a fact of life whose implications are staggering, and words such as "net" and "web" have taken on meanings no one would have understood less than two decades ago. It may be the most revolutionary mode of communication since the invention of radio, and some suggest it is the greatest leap forward since printing itself. We believe such claims are at least somewhat exaggerated. However, there is no question that the vast availability of information on the World Wide Web has made a profound impact on research in history and in many other fields of study. Anybody with a World Wide Web connection can set up a Web page, and so Web pages abound from individuals—from enthusiasts for this or that cause or celebrity, either living or dead. Naturally enough, various fanaticisms thrive in this uncontrolled electronic environment. If you want to post a Web page and maintain that you were abducted by space aliens who introduced you to Abraham Lincoln in another galaxy, nothing can stop you. Given the variety of American society, you will probably get a following who will tell you about their own conversations with Lincoln in outer space. Realizing this leads many people to doubt the value of the Web for serious academic research.

But many valuable and important resources are also on the Web, and they are growing. To help you harness this potential, Internet entrepreneurs have created a wide array of *search engines*—some with enticing names such as Excite, Infoseek, and GoTo—that connect you with subjects on the Web. These search engines allow you a blank space where you can type in keywords related to your inquiry. The engine will search for a while and present you with a list of "hits," as they are usually called, locations on the Web where at least one of those keywords is in the title or among the indexing words entered by that Web site's creator. There is a wide variety of these search engines, but you must realize that none of them, even the so-called metaengines that claim to utilize multiple individual search engines, actually will connect you to all the materials available. In fact, the operating parameters of most online search engines are frequently changing. Some that we previously recommended to students no longer seem to be as effective, and new search engines are appearing regularly. So rather than naming some that may be less useful by the time you read this, we simply suggest you try several different ones as you begin your project. A useful link to nearly fifty possibilities can presently be found at <http://www.etsu.edu/cas/history/search.htm>.

As with your keyword searches in online library catalogs, you will almost always need to refine your World Wide Web search in some way. If, for example, you type the word "Luther" in your search engine, the hits will include material on Martin Luther (the German religious reformer of the sixteenth century), several colleges that bear Luther's name, Martin Luther King, Jr. (the U.S. civil rights leader of the 1950s and 1960s), and probably a dozen or so people named Luther Jones or Luther Smith who have produced Web documents on the dangers of granulated sugar or on new cures for baldness. And you will likely waste time if you enter such words as "Rome," "Renaissance," "Italy," "modern," or "printing" in your search engine. Unfortunately, the ways to refine your online Web searches are even more varied than those for library catalogs. But as we advised when discussing them, the time you take to locate and read the "help" screens and learn how to focus your search will be repaid many times over.

Likely as not, all of these efforts to locate potential sources for your essay will have led you to a large number of possibilities—books, articles, Web sites, and other types of materials, including collections of primary sources. But even at this stage, you have not done all the preliminary work necessary to help in crafting your essay. You must still tap into the best of these sources to find the material that will give your essay substance. Now you must actually do the research! But remember our earlier advice: You may suppose that historians invariably follow these steps neatly one after the other. Not so! In practice, things seldom run so smoothly. Historians may begin with one topic, discover another when they do research, and change their minds again when they start writing. As they write, they may redefine their topic, and as they redefine the topic, they do more research. Writing your thoughts down often reveals gaps in your knowledge. Go back to your research to fill in these gaps. And again you will have to examine and analyze these newfound sources.

This entire process, as we have suggested at the beginning of this chapter, necessarily will involve hard work. We have found that our students often underestimate the amount of time and work involved. So, our advice is that you should take extra care to begin work as soon as possible on your essay and that you work steadily on the project. Postponing, even trying to bypass, the initial stages—or any of the other steps in the process leading to your final essay—will seldom yield results that will satisfy you, or your instructor.

DOING RESEARCH

As you move from gathering information about potential sources to analyzing those sources, you must also evaluate them. Your first touchstone, of course, will be to see if they actually relate to the topic you have chosen. If you have carefully crafted questions about your topic, you should be able to dismiss some potential sources relatively quickly. In fact, you may discard some even as you are continuing to locate others.

If you are fortunate to have access to a large and comprehensive library, you may find that many of the books and articles you have come upon are readily available. Some you may need to view in microform editions. Although these are not as convenient—nor as comforting to some researchers—as printed paper versions, they do offer a form of access welcome to a patient historian. If you have not often used a microfilm, -fiche, or -card reader, learn to do so. In many libraries it is essential if you wish to read at least some of the materials you have located. You may also have the option of requesting *interlibrary loan* privileges to obtain a book or article not available in your library. You may find that a good interlibrary-loan librarian is just as helpful in your research as the friendly reference librarian we mentioned previously. It has certainly been true in our experience.

Even as you move back and forth between gathering, analyzing, organizing, and presenting the information for your essay, you need to keep the evaluation principles of the historian's critical method in mind. As we noted when discussing evaluating materials in Chapter 2, you must first establish that all of your sources are plausible and trustworthy, and then if they are accurate and can be corroborated. For some of your sources this may be easier than for others.

Secondary Sources

Secondary sources will frequently be of two general sorts: articles and books. Applying the historian's critical method is somewhat different in each case. For example, the articles you locate in major professional journals will have, for the most part, passed through a process of peer review. Other historians will have read the articles before they were published, applying the essential elements of critical method. Their judgments will be a good start to making your own.

This is particularly fortunate because literally hundreds of such periodicals deal with history. Some journals publish articles about particular facets of history—the Middle Ages, military affairs, science, art, women—or the history of particular parts of the world—France, Africa, the Middle East, Malawi. Others, such as the *American Historical Review* and the *Journal of World History*, have a scope as wide as the discipline itself. An hour or two spent consulting the annual indexes of periodicals in their printed form or on a full-text journals storage database, such as JSTOR, can open your eyes to many issues that touch on your subject. And since the essays you write in a history course are more like journal articles than books, the journals will provide models of writing and thinking that you can imitate.

Among the secondary sources you have located there will also be books, and many of those available in your library. Most will also have been subject to some sort of critical evaluation, if not in the publication process then at least in their selection to be a part of the library's collections. That should give you some comfort. But since you will not limit your search simply to books directly about your topic, you will still need to make certain critical judgments. If you are writing about Woodrow Wilson, you will no doubt look for books that deal with his times. You may consult books about World War I, about the progressive era that Wilson represented, about people close to him, and about various issues in which he was involved. In such works you would look up the name, "Wilson, Woodrow" in the index and turn to those pages to see how Wilson is mentioned. You will need to satisfy yourself in each of these cases that what is written about Wilson is both plausible and trustworthy, and that it is accurate and may be corroborated. If you can satisfy yourself on these counts, you may discover yourself on the trail of a valuable insight.

Book reviews may also help you in evaluating some of your sources. Many historical journals and even some Web sites provide reviews of books. Among the latter, the H-Net Reviews at <http://www2.h-net.msu.edu/reviews> are particularly valuable, especially for books published in recent years. Some indexes to periodical literature include book reviews, but you should also look in *Book Review Digest*, which has provided a guide to published book reviews for nearly a century. You search for reviews by the names of book authors, usually in the years immediately after they were first published. While the *Digest* includes some academic journals, it also includes more popular reviews for an intelligent reading public. But these sorts of book reviews may also contain valuable insights about your potential source. A reviewer will tell you whether the book repeats old information, breaks new ground, contradicts received interpretations, and often whether the book is well written or else written in the style of some insurance policies—almost impossible to understand.

Occasionally reviews can be fiercely polemical, displaying historians at their worst. But then some books deserve to be attacked because they ignore scholarly evidence and present a one-sided view of their subject, often with a view of making a saint of someone who fell abysmally short of sanctity. More often, uncivil reviews reveal pettiness and sometimes jealousy, and it is unfortunately often true that historians with radically new insights into a historical problem may be pummeled by old believers who think the truth was discovered long ago. Still there is hardly any better way to be introduced to the historical profession than by reading lots and lots of book reviews. You should by all means read as many reviews of the same book—especially your potential sources—as you can, since different scholars will highlight different aspects of a book. You will often pick up information that you would otherwise miss and then be in a better position to evaluate the book as a source.

Primary Sources

Good history essays always refer to primary as well as to secondary sources. Be on the lookout for editions of the works by the various people who may enter your paper. Using texts written by those you write about gives your own work authority. When you use any edition of collected or selected works, check the dates of publication. Sometimes several different editions have been published of the same works. Usually, but not always, the best editions are the latest. These editions may be of different sorts. The most valuable are editions of the complete works in which every surviving text is collected and indexed, sometimes with other materials from the time the person lived. These can be important to determine the different views of your subject either over time or when addressing different audiences.

Also read published (and, if they are available to you, unpublished) autobiographies, but be skeptical of them. Apply the same critical historical standards you would for any other source: Is the account plausible, trustworthy, accurate, and can it be corroborated? Remember, when people write anything about themselves, they have a natural desire to put themselves in the best possible light for posterity. Autobiographies and memoirs almost always have a lot of fiction in them. Still, all of them contain some truth—although some are more truthful than others. Also look for collections of speeches or sermons, published diaries, and editions of correspondence, all of which are also fairly common.

Most historians enjoy reading such sources because, like photographs, they give us a sense of intimacy with bygone times and people we have not known. Like photographs, speeches, diaries, and letters are frequently datable. You can quickly see that they belong to a certain time and place, and in the eternal flux of things, they seem to make time stand still for a moment. Sermons and speeches can give you a sense of the public image and message someone wanted to convey. Diaries and collections of letters, on the other hand, frequently give us people in relatively unguarded prose, commenting on daily life without the caution that marks more public utterances. The private persona or personality of the diarist or letter writer may be different from the public image displayed in speeches or writing intended for a large audience.

In every case, though, you will need to apply your standards of historical criticism. Are the claims plausible, and are there reasons for you to treat them as trustworthy? For example, are you reading a copy of the letter saved by the author or one collected by the recipient? Despite the best of intentions, these are not always exactly the same. Keep that in mind, although you may have no choice but to use whatever version is available. Also consider if any claims or assertions made are accurate. Can you corroborate them from other sources?

Other editions of various sources relating to a general topic are also frequently collected and published. One of the most monumental of these is *The War of the Rebellion: A Compilation of the Official Records of the Union and Confederate Armies*, published in seventy volumes and now available and searchable electronically at <http://moa.cit.cornell.edu/moa/browse.monographs/waro.html>. This vast resource almost seems to contain a transcription of nearly every scrap of paper exchanged within the armies on both sides in the Civil War. (The noise of battle during the Civil War was so tremendous that men under fire could not hear each other speak. Therefore written orders carried from place to place on the battlefield were much more common than in earlier wars, and thousands of these were collected by the editors.)

We could list literally hundreds of additional examples of primary-source collections that can help you in research. Whatever your topic, check to see if your library has a collection of published documents related to your paper. When you search the catalog by keyword for your topic, use "sources" or "personal narratives" as an additional parameter; those are the principal terms used in Library of Congress subject headings to indicate primary-source materials. Browse through the collections you find even if you don't at first see that they are related to your topic. You may be pleasantly surprised. But remember always to examine critically the primary sources that you do find.

Your own college library probably has an archive or manuscript department with collections of unpublished letters, diaries, memos, and other materials. Look for them and see if there might be material related to your topic. There's nothing quite so thrilling as to look at the basic raw materials of history preserved in such sources. Many libraries and archives now also include oral history collections, tapes, and records of people—both well known and obscure—discussing the past and their participation in events then. You can sometimes learn something by the tone of voice people use to describe past events, although other interviews may only be available in written transcripts. In either case, interviews are valuable for studies of recent or fairly recent history. If, for example, you write about some aspect of combat in World War II, you can find many veterans to tell you of their experiences, giving you a firsthand view of history. The same is true of the civil rights movement in the United States, the Vietnam War, the Great Depression, the Jewish Holocaust in Europe, and many other events within memory of witnesses and participants still alive.

People who participated in great events or lived through particularly interesting times are often eager to talk about them. Don't be afraid to write or telephone people to ask for an interview. However, it is always best to conduct such interviews in person. Prepare for the interview by learning all you can about the person and by writing out questions beforehand. But don't be mechanically bound to your list before the interview begins. Explore each question thoroughly. Listen to your source, and be prepared to ask for clarification of details. If possible, record your interview on audio or videotape; if not, be sure to take extensive notes.

The gratifications of using all of these methods of inquiry into original primary sources are immense. Historians who have worked in the archives or who have heard the actual voices of witnesses to history experience a satisfaction that can hardly be described. Reading the original letters or papers written by women and men, famous or obscure, can give you a sense of the personal imprint each left of themselves. At some point every student of history, whether amateur or professional, should have the pleasure of looking at such a source and practicing the use of the historian's critical method to evaluating these materials.

Remember, too, that primary sources can also include photographs, paintings, sculpture, and architecture. Professor Liana Vardi's fine 1996 article, "Imagining the Harvest in Early Modern Europe," considers representations of peasants by artists for three centuries after 1500. She shows that gradually the peasants, the farmers who worked the fields, disappear from paintings of rural landscapes. By comparing paintings with poetry from the time, she argues that city dwellers and aristocrats became afraid of peasants, who frequently revolted against the harsh conditions of their lives. Then, in the eighteenth century, peasants returned to paintings, where they appear docile and obedient and happy[2]. The paintings, reproduced in black and white throughout the article, serve as essential primary sources. You, too, may find important visual sources for papers you write.

Finally, when considering primary sources for your essay, Professor Vardi's article should remind you not to dismiss the possibilities of literature—poetry, short stories, and novels—which often capture the tenor and tone of the time in which they were written. While literary sources are sometimes difficult to interpret, particularly given the sometimes metaphorical and even personal expressions of the authors, in many cases the connections to a historical topic are clear enough. Consider, for example, this 1899 poem, "Take Up the White Man's Burden," by the well known Anglo-Indian Rudyard Kipling, which he specifically headed "The United States and the Philippine Islands":

> Send forth the best ye breed—
> Go bind your sons to exile
>   To serve your captives' need;
> To wait in heavy harness
>   On fluttered folk and wild—

---

2 Liana Vardi. 1996. "Imagining the Harvest in Early Modern Europe," *American Historical Review* 101:1357–1397.

Your new caught, sullen peoples,
   Half devil and half child.

  . . . .

Take up the White Man's burden—
   Ye dare not stoop to less—
Nor call too loud on Freedom
   To cloak your weariness;
By all ye cry or whimper,
   By all ye leave or do,
The silent, sullen peoples
   Shall weigh your Gods and you.[3]

Were you writing an essay on United States imperialism—or on imperialism and colonialism in general—the importance of this poem as a primary source should be clear. These brief verses capture some essential expressions of the colonialist mentality and if nothing else could lend an added dimension to your essay on the subject. Frequently you may come across literary works, perhaps some not as well known as Kipling, which can serve to enliven what you write. You might need to do some additional reading to make certain your interpretation is not too far from the mark. Consider that effort, too, a part of the evaluation process necessary as you use your sources to write any history essay.

Internet Sources

Strictly speaking, Internet sources are not different from primary and secondary sources. They do not really constitute a separate category of historical materials. Both primary and secondary sources for writing about history can be found in abundance on the World Wide Web. But as we have mentioned previously, and as you are

---

[3] Rudyard Kipling, "Take Up the White Man's Burden," in *A Choice of Kipling's Verse*, ed. T. S. Eliot (New York: Anchor Books, 1941), 143–144. There are many editions available.

certainly aware, the nature of the World Wide Web is such that literally anybody can create a Web page and post literally anything for the entire world (at least potentially) to see. Many scholars applaud these developments as a further democratization of information. Certainly the role of a careful, and sometimes overcautious, journal or book editor is bypassed in the case of many Web pages. So, too, is the role of the friendly reference librarian (although many of them are now willing to point questioning students to valuable Web pages as well as more traditional reference materials).

If you have an Internet address for a Web page, technically referred to as a URL (uniform resource locator), you can visit the Web site when you type that URL into your Web browser. There are many listings, even entire books, of important or especially valuable URLs for college history students. These are designed to help you in making the necessary evaluations of Web sites as a part of your research process. We have previously recommended several to students in our classes and in the third edition of this book. One of our favorites, originally conceived as a broad collection of both primary and secondary historical sources, was the Hanover Historical Texts Project maintained at Hanover College in Indiana. Still found at <http://history.hanover.edu/texts.html>, the Historical Texts Project has been cut back drastically in scope since July 2000, with many fewer entries than were once available. And the Historical Text Archive, originally developed at Mississippi State University, has moved twice since the third edition of this book appeared. As this fourth edition is being readied for publication, it can now be found at <http://historicaltextarchive.com/>. There it continues to offer a superb collection of documents, essays, images, and related material in many fields of history—as well as advertising logos, which became necessary to ensure its continued support.

Our experience, and that of our students, with these two Web sites—as well as numerous others—offers an important caveat about using the World Wide Web for historical research. Web sites are changing all the time, and almost any list of excellent Web resources may soon be obsolete. Of course everyone knows that books, too, disappear, not least by extensive use. And archives may be destroyed in catastrophic events such as fire or through neglect. But somehow the transitory nature of the World Wide Web often looms as a larger problem in a historian's mind. It is not yet a substitute for a good library. Do not let this concern lead you to avoid using it entirely. Use the Web cautiously. Take full advantage of the powers of available search engines to locate potential materials. Keep good records of what you find. And always go back to any site at least one additional time to be sure you have recorded the URL and other information correctly. Also learn to recognize that some problems in locating—and relocating—Web materials may be caused not at the source of the Web site but somewhere in the chain of transmission to the computer you are using.

Certainly be skeptical about what you find, as you should be when considering any historical source. In the case of the World Wide Web materials, though, the role of historical evaluation has passed from such designated mediators as librarians and editors directly to the researcher and writer. In short, it is *your* responsibility to assess the value of the materials you locate on the Internet. Quite likely your instructor will expect you to "be more cautious and evaluative in an electronic environment"[4] as you prepare your history essays. This is not unreasonable. But if you follow our general advice on evaluating materials presented in Chapter 2 and make use of the Writer's Checklist included there, you should have few difficulties in doing so. Applying those principles to your Internet research will be excellent practice in developing your skills at using the historian's critical method.

If you have begun the process of gathering information for your essay by establishing clear questions you wish to answer, you

---

[4] Deborah Lines Anderson, "Heuristics for the Educational Use and Evaluation of Electronic Information," in *History.edu: Essays on Teaching with Technology*, ed. Dennis A. Trickle and Scott M. Merriman (Armonk, NY: M. E. Sharpe, 2001), 135.

will be well on the way to an evaluation strategy once you turn to the World Wide Web. Similarly, if you have done a little background work ahead of time, you will have a better basis of information to use in assessing what you find on the Web. From this foundation you can begin the process of using the historian's critical method. First, ask yourself: Is what I have found plausible? Just as we have said before, the more fantastic the information and explanations you are offered seem to be, the more likely they will be simply fantasy. Once past that examination, consider whether the Web site should be considered trustworthy. You can begin to do this by going to the home page of the Web site you have found. In some cases you will see a link "home" which you may choose. Or you may follow back the URL given on your Web browser for the site you have found. Try using just the letters beginning on the left of your browser's location bar up until the first single slash (/) as a separate URL. This may not always be successful, although it will frequently take you to the home or foundation site where the materials you have located reside.

Once you get to the home page for the material you want, you will have to start asking questions again. Who created and/or maintains this site? What organization, if any, sponsors this work? Do they have any particular interests in the content? Or, are there no sponsors? Is this the work of a single enthusiast? Certainly individuals may create such Web materials for many scholarly or nonpartisan purposes. You may need to use the historian's skill of inference, which we also discussed in Chapter 2, in trying to answer some of these questions, at least in part. But if you are unable to locate any information about the sponsor or creator of a Web page, that should give you pause. You likely will question the trustworthiness of the information you have found. If you use it at all for your essay, you will want to do so with great caution.

Next, you will want to think about the accuracy of the information you have found on the Web site. Although some historical information is almost timeless, you may make a start in thinking about accuracy by determining when the site was created and how recently it may have been updated. Even historians want to know if the information they are using reflects the most recent research. Consequently, many Web sites with historical information will clearly indicate—on the Web site itself—the dates of their most recent revisions or upgrades. Even where this is not obvious, you may sometimes be able to determine a most recently modified date when you are using the Netscape Web browser. With the Web site in view on your computer screen, use your mouse to select "View" from the main taskbar, and then "Page Info" from the dropdown menu. The information you will see may include details of the "last modified" date for that particular Web page. But since the Internet Explorer Web browser does not support the same information, and therefore some Web sites do not record such information, you may not be able to locate it using either Explorer or Netscape.

Do not despair or reject the information out of hand if you cannot find its most recently modified date. You can look for other indicators of accuracy. Read carefully to see if there are lots of categorical assertions. Claims of *completely*, *never*, or *always*—as opposed to, say, *nearly*, *seldom*, or *usually*—can also be indicators that the authors may not have explored all the ramifications of the topic. Also look for the qualities of impartiality and balance in the writing. Has the author taken other opinions into account? As we have said before, that is one of the markers of good historical writing. Not only should you write dispassionately, you should also expect to find that quality in any Web pages you might want to rely on for information to support your essay. And finally, you might also assess the accuracy of the information you find on the Web by looking for corroboration in other sources. In doing so, you should again follow the suggestions we made in Chapter 2. While it is not necessary to reject information that you may not be able to affirm through other sources, you will certainly need to treat it more cautiously in what you write.

As you use all of these means to assess information you find on the World Wide Web, remember that you are practicing the essential evaluative skills necessary for being a historian. No matter whether your sources are primary or secondary, oral or written, found on the web or in a print medium—the essence of the historian's critical method remains the same. Making a conscious effort to apply it to your research work will also help you to improve the writing in your completed history essay.

TAKING NOTES AND WRITING DRAFTS

■ ■ ■

Although every respectable historian knows the importance of gathering information before completing a historical essay, most also know how important it is to begin the writing process as early as possible. In reality, this is a form of practice. Pianists do finger exercises before they play. Baseball players take batting practice before a game. These activities help them limber up for the real thing. Similar exercises will help you prepare to write. Maintaining such a view of the writing process will also help you avoid some common, and often recurring, myths about writing.

One such myth is that writers are inspired, that real writers turn out articles and books and reports with the greatest of ease. Another is that if you must write several drafts of anything, you are not a good writer. Still another is that if you labor to get on paper what you want to say, you will not improve it much if you write a second or even a third draft. We can well attest that none of these is really true in practice. While every writer has a different approach to the process, for none is that process quick and easy. As we wrote at the beginning of the last chapter, all writing—if it is done well—is hard work.

For example, few writers manage to write without revising. The almost unanimous testimony of good writers in all disciplines is that writing is always difficult and that they must write several drafts to be satisfied with an essay or a book. The easier writing is to read, the harder it has been for the writer to produce it. Your final draft must express a clear understanding of your own thoughts. But the way to that understanding may lead through several drafts. Writing, rereading, and revising clarifies your thoughts and strengthens your hold on your own idea. Once you have gone through that process, you have an essay that cannot be blown away by the first person who comes along with a firm opinion.

If you start writing early in the process, the great values of rewriting will be clearer to you. As you take notes during a lecture or discussion, do not let your writing stop there. Afterwards, write a brief summary of the important points made during the class, and jot down all the questions that come to mind about what has been said. That process alone may lead you back to update certain sections of your notes. It will likely lead you as well to formulate further ideas about what you have just heard. As we suggested in the last chapter, such a writing habit may also produce a personal treasure trove of topics for future history papers.

It is also usually good to start writing soon after you get an assignment. Do *not* attempt to make this preliminary writing a complete rough draft. Simply set down your thoughts about the topic you have been given or—drawing upon the collection of potential topics you have already made—about brief ideas concerning the topics you might write about in completing the assignment. You can begin by merely jotting a few words or phrases or sentences without trying to work them into paragraphs. Gradually, you may continue forming disconnected paragraphs that allow you to work out your ideas. They, in turn, will stir your mind to more thoughts.

Inexperienced writers often assume that an accomplished writer does all the research first and then writes. On the contrary, most experienced writers find that no matter how much they know about a subject at the start, the act of writing confronts them with new problems and new questions, gives them new leads, sends them off in search of more information to pursue those new leads, and sometimes results in conclusions different from those with which they began. For the experienced writer, the writing proceeds in a process of leaping forward and leaping back, but above all involves some sort of writing very early and continues until the essay is completed.

To postpone writing until one has done all the possible research on the subject can be disastrous. Many historians have fallen before the demand they put on themselves to read one more book or article before they could start writing. That was the fate of Frederick Jackson Turner, who, after propounding his "frontier thesis" of American history, was expected to write many important books. He signed several contracts with publishers without being able to produce the books. Historian Richard Hofstadter wrote the following sad words about Turner. They should be stamped on the skin of every historian tempted to put off writing:

> He became haunted by the suspicion, so clear to his biographer, that he was temperamentally "incapable of the sustained effort necessary to complete a major scholarly volume." "I hate to write," he blurted out to a student in later years, "it is almost impossible for me to do so." But it was a self-description arrived at after long and hard experience. In 1901 when he was forty, Turner had signed contracts for nine books, not one of which was ever to be written and only a few of which were even attempted, and his life was punctuated by an endless correspondence with disappointed publishers. For an academic family, the Turners lived expensively and entertained generously, and the income from any of the textbooks he promised to write would have been welcome, but the carrot of income was no more effective than the stick of duty and ambition. Turner's teaching load at Wisconsin was for a time cut down, in the hope that it would clear the way for his productive powers, but what it produced was only a misunderstanding with university trustees. Turner's reluctance to address himself to substantive history was so overwhelming that A. B. Hart, a martinet of an editor who presided with ruthless energy over the authors of the American Nation series, extracted *Rise of the New West* out of him only by dint of an extraordinary series of nagging letters and bullying telegrams. Hart in the end counted this his supreme editorial achievement. "It ought to be carved on my tombstone that I was the only man in the world that secured what might be called an adequate volume from Turner," he wrote to Max Farrand; and Farrand, one of Turner's closest friends who watched his agonized efforts to produce his last unfinished volume in the splendid setting provided by the

Huntington Library, sadly concluded that he would not have finished it had he lived forever.

Over the years Turner had built up a staggering variety of psychological and mechanical devices, familiar to all observers of academia, to stand between himself and the finished task. There was, for example, a kind of perfectionism, which sent him off looking for one more curious fact or decisive bit of evidence, and impelled the elaborate rewriting of drafts that had already been rewritten. There were the hopelessly optimistic plans for what he would do in the next two or twelve or eighteen months, whose inevitable nonfulfillment brought new lapses into paralyzing despair. There was an undisciplined curiosity, an insatiable, restless interest in *everything*, without a correspondingly lively determination to consummate anything; a flitting from one subject to another, a yielding to the momentary pleasures of research as a way of getting further from the discipline of writing. ("I have a lot of fun exploring, getting lost and getting back, and telling my companions about it," he said, but "telling" here did not mean writing.) There was over-research and overpreparation with the consequent inability to sort out the important from the trivial—a small mountain of notes, for example, gathered for a trifling projected children's book of 25,000 words on George Rogers Clark. There were, for all the unwritten books, thirty-four large file drawers bulging with notes on every aspect of American history. There were elaborate maps, drawn to correlate certain forces at work in American politics. There were scrapbooks, and hours spent filling them in. . . . There were, of course, long letters of explanation to publishers, and other letters setting forth new plans for books. There was indeed an entire set of letters to Henry Holt and Company, examining various possible titles for the last unfinishable volume—letters that the exasperated publishers finally cut off by suggesting that the matter might well wait until the book itself became a reality.[1]

Turner's life helps illustrate something we said earlier in this book: Writing history is brave business. At some point you have to settle down and do it, and doing it takes a kind of courage that every historian must summon up if he or she is to do the job.

---

[1] Richard Hofstadter, *The Progressive Historians* (New York: Knopf, 1968), 115–117.

RECORDING IDEAS AND INFORMATION

As we have suggested, you should start the writing process early. When you read background information for your essay, keep brief notes with location information, including URLs for web sources and page numbers for books and articles. You do not have to write extensive notes. The location details will help you find the information again when you need it. Write down questions about what you read. (We scribble copious notes and questions in the margins of our own books. But never, NEVER write in a library book!) There are many ways to keep such notes. For years we recommended that our students take notes on 3 × 5 note cards or keep a separate notebook for each project. Either were easy to carry in a briefcase or book bag, and we found them to be more convenient than loose tablets of paper. In recent years we have come to rely more on our computers for note-taking as well as writing, although some researchers remain more comfortable with cards or notebooks.

Whatever format you select, the main point is to take notes even as you begin your investigations. Ask yourself questions, type or jot down significant phrases, and note places where historians disagree on the subject you are pursuing. Pay attention to what one historian notices that another ignores. One writer may write much about Luther's hostility to Jews; another may ignore the subject altogether. Why? Make notes of your own opinions about both the historians and the material. Even in the early stages of your research, important ideas may pop into your head. Write them down, and test them with further study. You may discover that further research confirms that some of your first impressions are gems.

We recommend you consider using a computer if you can. Computers add facility to note taking, allowing you to search your notes by keyword, cross-reference the information you have found, and sometimes even create citations. At the time we are writing this, one free program we particularly find useful is "Scribe," created by Elena Razlogova of George Mason University's Center for History and the New Media. It is available as a free download from the World Wide Web at <http://chnm.gmu.edu/staff/elena/Notes/index.html> in a compressed file format. You will need to use an "unzip" program to decompress the "Scribe" program and its attachments before you can begin work. (If you need help doing so, go to <www.etsu.edu/cas/history/noteprog.htm> for some assistance.) It takes a little time to study the instructions and master the "Scribe" program operations, although if you anticipate using it for several projects, we think it will be well worth your time and effort.

But almost any word-processing program can be used for note taking. Be sure to indicate clearly [perhaps in brackets] location information, particularly Web links or pages numbers, as you copy notes into a computer file. And if you take care—as you should in all note-taking endeavors—to include keywords, you can later locate them by using the search function on your word-processing program. Many programs will also allow you to shift your notes to the file holding your essay when you begin to write; simply block and copy text from your note files, then open your essay file and paste the information there. Whether you use a specialized note-taking or database program, or merely take notes with your word-processing program, be sure to save your notes as you work and especially as you finish each research or writing session, no matter how short. Keep several copies, using both your computer hard drive as well as removable disks. In preparing this book, for example, we have kept copies of each chapter in a separate file, and we have four or more copies of each—on our computer hard drives, floppy disks, and even a compressed "Zip" disk.

Review your notes at the end of each day. When you go over your notes, you sometimes begin to see connections that you didn't make at first. By continually reviewing your notes you also impress them on your memory. Short-term memory is flighty. You can read something, be intensely engaged in it, and take notes about it—but then forget it quickly if you don't do something to renew the experience. Reviewing notes fixes them in your mind and makes you remember them better so that you find them more easily among your thoughts when you start to write. Reviewing your notes daily will help you hold on to ideas that will then be nurtured by your subconscious powers of incubation, the almost miraculous ability of the mind to work while thinking of other things or even sleeping. Reading the notes over again will stir up thoughts that will contribute much to the final conception of your paper, and such reading will clarify the method you use to approach that goal.

Always include bibliographical references in your notes. Be sure to include the essential elements for any such reference: *authorship* (and also the names of editors and/or translators); the *title* (or titles, in the case of, say, an article in a book or journal); the *location* where you found the information (including place of publication or, in the case of Internet information, the URL, and, when appropriate, volume and page numbers); and the *date*(s) of publication or access. It is not necessary to follow the conventions for note or bibliographic forms at this time, but it is very important to be sure you include all the essential details. For example:

```
Hyatt, Irwin T., Our Ordered Lives Confess,
Cambridge, Mass. and London: Harvard University
Press, 1976.
```

Later on you can refer in your notes simply to the author and use a page number, "Hyatt, 27" to locate your source of information. If you use several books, articles, or other sources by the same author, give the author and an abbreviated form of the title for your notes. Instead of giving the full bibliographic information for Woodrow Wilson's *History of the American People*, for example, you can write, "Wilson, *History,* 4, 160" (to indicate page 160 in the fourth volume in the set). Your main principle should be this: *Be sure you record where you got your information.* You must be able to refer accurately to your sources when you write; we will discuss more about this in Chapter 8. You will save yourself much grief if you keep track of your sources carefully while you do your research.

In addition to bibliographic references, take three other kinds of notes as you do research. The first is direct quotation. *Always* place direct quotations within quotation marks in your notes, and copy the quotation accurately. Make accurate reference to the pages and/or the source of the quotation. You may want to put a heading on the note to help you remember why you took it down. Always review the quotation for accuracy once you have written it down. The eye and the hand can slip while you are looking first at your source and then at your notebook, card, or computer screen. When you type, fingers can go astray, typing one word when you mean another. It may help to put a check or asterisk (*) by the quotation to tell yourself that you have reviewed it for accuracy once you have put it down.

Here is a sample note showing direct quotation for an essay on Woodrow Wilson and black Americans. Be sure to use key words in your notes. If this were on your computer, you could retrieve it by using "KKK" in your heading and using the search function of your word-processing program to bring it up when you needed it. You could then easily append it to your essay. If it were on cards, you could put the keyword at the top of the card; or you might write the keyword in the margin of a project notebook.

```
         Wilson mocks fears by blacks of the KKK
   *  "It threw the negroes into a very ecstasy of panic
   to see these sheeted 'ku klux' move near them in the
   shrouded night; and their comic fear stimulated the
   lads who excited it to many an extravagant prank and
   mummery. No one knew or could discover who the
   masked players were; no one could say whether they
   meant serious or only innocent mischief; and the
   zest of the business lay in keeping the secret
   close." Wilson, History: 5, 59-60
   ➜      Wilson seems to enjoy this fear, finds it
   comic. Regards early Klansmen as comic.
```

Avoid copying too much direct quotation in your notes. Writing down the quotation takes time, and you can easily make errors in transcribing it. You save time while you exercise your mind by summary or paraphrase rather than by direct quotation. (Or, if you have the book only for a limited time, such as on interlibrary loan, you may wish to photocopy some pages relevant to your work if you must send the book back before you write the paper.) Paraphrasing is especially valuable, as it opens your mind to the possibilities of how you might present the information.

As you write, you will probably have Wilson's volumes easily available. When you look at your notes, you can return to the original source (or your photocopies) and quote it exactly, word for word. Or, to save space, you may say something like this: "Wilson mocked the fear blacks had of the Klan," and you would put in a note the place where the mockery might be found. Here is an example of a summary note:

> ➤   Wilson mocks blacks' fears of KKK. Seems to enjoy the terror of blacks before the KKK and to regard early Klansmen as pranksters. Wilson, *History*, 5, 59–60

The third kind of note is your own comment when you read. Comment often as you make notes. Commenting requires you to reflect on what you read, making you an active rather than a passive reader. Be sure to distinguish between the notes that are your own thoughts and notes that are direct quotations or summaries of your sources. We often put an arrow before our own thoughts (as we have indicated in the previous examples), whether we are using cards, a notebook, or our computers. The arrow lets us know that these thoughts are ours. If you do not take care in distinguishing your thoughts from the thoughts of your source, you may be accused of plagiarism. As we explained in Chapter 1, that is a very serious matter and one from which few authors can easily recover.

Here is an example of how you might enter a note about your own thoughts:

> ➤   Wilson's view of the Klan goes hand in hand with his general view that blacks have no

right to be free of fear or to take part as
citizens in the United States. His mention of the
"comic" fear of blacks suggests an unconscious
appropriation of the common stereotypes, that
blacks were either funny or dangerous and in any
case that their fears were not to be taken
seriously. He barely suggests in the *History* that
Klansmen often beat blacks, burned their houses,
and sometimes killed them. For Wilson, blacks are
always mistreated by *Northerners*. Northerners
always mistreat blacks by asking them to assert
themselves. Wilson sees blacks as being most happy
when they are submissive. He seems to have no sense
of the dignity that blacks might lose by being so
regarded. *History*, 5, 59-60

The purpose of such a note is to keep your mind active as you read. A note like this can help shape a major idea for the paper that you will write.

ORGANIZING YOUR ESSAY

Such note taking will help you begin brainstorming, that is, putting your mind to work at a task through a playful, intense process of forcing out your thoughts. In brainstorming you may jot down ideas one after another as fast as you can think of them, knowing that you may reject most of them. You might also brainstorm with groups of fellow students by talking hard at each other, trying out ideas, and tossing them out to friends and colleagues to see how they fare in open discussion. Brainstorming is an excellent way to arrive at or focus your topic for a history paper.

By the time you have spent two or three afternoons refining your subject, gathering your bibliography, and doing some reading, you will begin to feel more confident about your knowledge. You will have left the somewhat flat and limited accounts of the encyclopedias and other reference books, and you will have started looking at primary sources and specialized books and articles. It is these latter sources that you will want to document in your essay. Your reading should have suggested interesting approaches to your topic. You should have asked questions along the way, writing them down in your notes. You will have noticed patterns or repeated ideas in your research.

Sometimes a pattern occurs in a consistent response to certain subjects. For example, Woodrow Wilson defended the South in writing and in speeches. Why did he do that, and what effect did this attitude have on American history? You may have started with the resolve to write a paper about Woodrow Wilson. If you were lucky, you thought of a limited topic right away, one you might do in ten or fifteen pages. Perhaps, however, you were not able to limit your topic enough. Make a list of interesting topics or problems relating to Wilson. Keep working at it until you arrive at something manageable. The following notes illustrate this attempt to produce both something interesting and something you can do in the time and space available.

> "The Civil War in Woodrow Wilson's *History of the American People.*" Too vague. Too many topics possible.
> "Wilson's Defense of the Ku Klux Klan in his *History of the American People.*" Not bad. Wilson's defense of the KKK is surprising, given the popular view that he was liberal for his time. But maybe too narrow. Wilson defends the Klan over several pages in his book. Only vague comments disapproving of Klan violence. No real indignation about that violence. Most of Wilson's *History* is vague. General statements throughout. Retells more of what he felt and believed about the facts rather than what the facts were. Not an impressive piece of work.

The temptation might be to go from Wilson to some general background information about the Klan itself. Then you have to ask questions like these: Do I have the primary sources to study the Klan? Is the topic too big for a paper in my course? Wilson's sympathetic words for the Klan provoke other ideas. What was Wilson's attitude towards blacks in the South and in American society at large? Consult the index in several volumes of the Wilson papers. Slowly read Wilson's comments about blacks in various contexts. Here is much information, and you begin to see patterns. Wilson has no sympathy for the efforts of blacks to vote after the Civil War. He never writes as if blacks and whites are equals. He favors segregation in the federal civil service, especially the Post Office. He insults black leaders who come to visit him at the White House. The major pattern seems clear: Wherever Wilson speaks of race, he assumes the inferiority of blacks and supports segregation.

Slowly an idea emerges. You adopt a provisional title: "Woodrow Wilson's Attitudes toward Black Americans." You can change a provisional title later. You can change anything in a paper at this stage, and your changes may be sweeping. While you use it, the provisional title gives direction to your work. That sense of direction will help you work faster and more efficiently because it helps organize your thoughts, making you evaluate information you have collected so you can make proper use of it.

If you have done your research well, you cannot use all the information you have collected in your notes. Good writing is done out of an abundance of knowledge. The provisional title will act as a filter in your mind, holding and organizing things you should keep for your essay and excluding information that will not contribute to your argument. And who knows? You may be able to use your surplus in papers you will write later in college or life! Once you arrive at a topic, focus your reading. If you plan to write about Woodrow Wilson's relation to blacks in America, limit yourself to reading only the parts of the Wilson papers and of books about Wilson relating to that subject. You may become so interested in Wilson that you continue to seek other information about him later on. Good! But while you write your paper, limit your reading to texts that help you to your goal. Maintaining that discipline will help you avoid the problems which plagued the famous historian Frederick Jackson Turner!

We would encourage you to write at least a brief outline to help organize your ideas and your evidence. Some writers sit down and start hammering on the keyboard without any clear idea of the steps they will take in developing their argument. If that process works for you, use it. But most people find it more efficient to shape their ideas before they begin to write a draft, and we have found that to be true in our writing. You can at least jot down a list of points you want to cover—a list that can be much more flexible than a detailed outline. You can rearrange items on your list as your intuitions suggest better forms of organization. Never be afraid to change a list or outline once you have begun. No matter how clearly you think you see your project in outline before you write a draft, writing may change your ideas. Be ready to follow your mind in its adventures with the evidence.

Here is an example of a rough outline for a paper on Woodrow Wilson's attitudes towards black Americans:

```
Argument: Wilson's attitudes towards blacks, a
mixture of paternalism and fear, contributed to
racial segregation introduced in the federal civil
service early in his presidential administration.
    1. William Monroe Trotter's interview with
       Wilson in November 1914 about segregation
    2. Larger meaning of the interview
    3. Wilson's reasons given to Trotter for
       accepting racial segregation
    4. Deeper explanation—Wilson's lifelong
       attitudes towards black Americans; things
       he said and wrote long before he became
       President of the United States
    5. Origins: Wilson's romantic view of the
       South and admiration for the Confederacy
    6. The attitudes expressed in his History of
       the American People
    7. Hostility toward blacks by white
       Southerners Wilson appointed to his Cabinet
```

```
8. Acceptance of racial segregation by the
   American people
9. Wilson's segregationist policies and their
   disastrous effect on race relations
```

A list outline such as this one avoids a proliferation of numbers and letters for headings and subheadings. You may add subheadings if you want, but you may not need them. Determining the sequence of your thoughts is likely sufficient. Indeed, sometimes worrying about the details of formal outlining—Roman numerals, large and small, and the placement of each point or subpoint within the outline—may distract you from the essential task: organizing your thoughts. But having made a list outline, such as this, you can more confidently write a first draft. In this case, you would have decided to shape an analytical narrative, telling a story and explaining its significance for American history. You will tell what happened, who is responsible, and why the story is important. Along the way you will tell when and where these happenings took place. And so you can begin.

WRITING DRAFTS

Leave yourself time enough to work on several drafts of your paper. If you start writing your paper the day before it is due, stay up all night to finish that first draft, and hand it in without having time to revise it, you do an injustice to yourself and your instructor. You may get by, but you may not be proud of your work, and the instructor will probably be bored with it. A hard-pressed instructor, sitting up for hours and hours reading and marking papers from everyone in the class (and yes, we have actually done this!), deserves your best effort.

Note that we are not saying you should avoid staying up all night long working on your paper before you hand it in. Many writers discover that they get an adrenaline flow from working steadily at a final draft for hours and hours before they give it up, and they may stay up all night because they are excited about their work and cannot leave it. We understand that feeling from our own writing adventures. Hearing the birds begin to sing outside at first light before dawn after working at our yellow pads or keyboard all night long is an experience we have both shared, and we have liked it. That kind of night comes when we have worked hard for a long time, perhaps for years, and feel in command of what we are doing and want to drive on to the end.

But no writer can produce consistently good work by waiting until the last minute to begin. Discipline yourself. When you start writing, stick to it for at least a couple of hours. You may not go very fast. You may consult your notes continually. You may become discouraged. But stay seated, and keep going. The most important task for you in writing your first draft is to actually write it! Get a beginning, a middle, and an end down on paper or on your computer. Write more than you need to write at first. If your assignment is to write a fifteen-page paper, make your first draft twenty pages. Pack in information. Use quotations. Ruminate about what you are describing. Ask yourself the now familiar questions about your paper, and try to answer them.

When you get your first draft into being, several things happen. You feel an immense relief. An unwritten assignment is more formidable than one you have written—even in a rough draft. You have some idea now what you can say in the space you have available. You have some idea of the major questions you want to address. You know some areas of weakness where you have to do further research. You can see which of your conclusions seem fairly certain and which seem shaky. You can see if you have an idea that binds all your data together into a thesis, a controlling motive that resolves or defines some puzzle that you find in your sources. You can now revise.

Revision proceeds in various ways. If you write with a computer and a word-processing program, you can bring your paper up on the screen and start working back through it, inserting, deleting, and changing around the order of the paper. (It's a good idea to make a separate backup copy of that first draft, giving it a different file name, so that if you cut something you later decide you want to restore, you can do so without pain.) Many writers like to print out a draft and go over it with a pen or pencil, making changes that they then type into the draft on the computer. Some behavioral research has shown that the longer people work with computers, the more they tend to do their revising directly from the screen without printing out. You have to use the method that suits you best.

The word-processing programs we use are invaluable for checking our spelling and grammar, but only against the words and grammatical phrases stored in their memories. We always read what we have written on the screen and study each of the errors identified by the program; most often we correct those the computer has spotted. But we also know that in the binary logic of the computer, some of our mistakes are not readily identified. If we have written *soul* when we mean the bottom of a shoe, for example, that will not be marked as an error. This is because the program's memory sees both *soul* and *sole* as correct and does not mark our writing slip as a mistake. There are many other examples. Therefore, after making revisions on our computer screens, we have come back to the practice of also printing out a manuscript, going over it carefully with pen or pencil, and only then inserting final corrections and revisions in the computer. You may wish to consider this approach as well, as it also may facilitate other steps in the revision process.

Perhaps the important part of the task is to read your work over many times. As you read, ask yourself questions. Be sure you consider, or reconsider, some of the steps you have already used in the process. Return to the ten principles for a good historical essay we introduced in Chapter 1 and use the Writer's Checklist we included there, making sure you examine each point carefully as you read your draft. Also consider some of the following supplemental questions while making your revisions:

1. Although you should have narrowed your topic already, does your essay in fact stick to the topic? Have you dealt with all of the essential issues? Have you shifted the ground or gone off on tangents?

2. Is the major motive for writing this essay clear? Have you made your essential point unambiguously? And do your supporting arguments and the evidence you use actually lead your reader to that conclusion?

3. Are your own views on the matter clearly evident? Have you used your powers of inference to present what you think instead of being content merely to report what you have found in your evidence?

4. Is your essay likely to interest readers? Have you begun in a manner that will catch the attention of readers? And do you lead them carefully through an understanding of the evidence toward the conclusions you want them to accept?

5. Have you used your evidence effectively? Does similar evidence appear in the same section of the essay so readers will not feel randomly jerked from one subject to another? Is there evidence missing for any segments of the essay?

6. Are the sources of the evidence clear to readers? Have you documented the evidence in a format that readers might use to find some of the same information themselves if they chose to do so? (See Chapter 8 for details concerning effective ways to do this.)

7. Have you been fair in presenting your evidence? Do you take contrary evidence into account? And is your tone consistent, and neither preachy nor belligerent? Do you sound more certain than you really are?

8. Do the conclusions mirror the opening in some way? Could someone who reads only the first and last paragraphs have a fairly good idea of what the essay is about and understand your point of view?

9. Is the writing clear? Are there any muddled sentences? Is the passive voice used in ways that obscure rather than clarify

who was responsible for the actions? Are words used appropriately? Do you avoid clichés and unnecessary words as well as needless repetition? (In Chapters 6 and 7, we consider some of these issues more fully.)

10. Will the essay be clear to your intended readers? Is there enough context for those unfamiliar with the subject? Or is there too much background detail so that some readers might assume they do not need to read the essay?

As we have already said, you can cultivate a good sense of revision by reading your own work again and again. Reading aloud helps. You can sometimes pick out rough places in your prose because they make you stumble in reading them. Reading aloud with inflection and expression will help you catch places where you may be misleading or confusing.

Professional writers often have others read their work and make suggestions about it. Get help from friends—as we have for every edition of this book. Do not ask them, "What do you think of my essay?" They will tell you it is good. Ask them instead, "What do you think I am saying in this paper?" You will sometimes be surprised by what comes out—and you will get some ideas for revision. Also ask them what they think you might do to improve your writing so that the essential points you want to make would be clear to them.

Some of you may also be involved in a peer editing process whereby students comment on drafts of each others' essays. Your college or university may encourage such collaborations, and/or your instructor may encourage you to do so. Or you may wish to form your own group—a kind of writing club—in which you will all help each other in revising your essays. There are a variety of approaches to this process. You could do well by simply using the Writer's Checklists in this book as a basis for commenting on your fellow students' papers. There are also a number of explanations and guides to peer editing. One that our students have found helpful is in "Writing at Guilford: An Online Manual," written for students at Guilford College by Jeff Jeske. Our students have retrieved it at <http://www.guilford.edu/original/writing_manual/> by selecting "Peer Editing" from the menu.

If you do take advantage of this frequently effective approach in your revisions, keep in mind that the purpose is to help one another, not to demonstrate how much more you may think you know about writing—or the topic of the essay—than the author. Similarly, Professor Jeske cautions:

> It is worth remembering that a major goal of peer editing is to enable writers to make effective revising decisions. Praise alone will not help; when it appears unalloyed, it suggests that the editor has not invested the necessary effort, not thought deeply about the paper's effects and the way the prose could be improved.
>
> Nevertheless, the tone of the editorial response should be positive. Don't merely point out what's wrong. Identify the things that the author has done well: this way the author will know what to continue to do. . . .
>
> The collective goal is that we all improve—and, as this happens, that we develop a positive attitude toward the activity in which we are engaged.[2]

Remember, a "critical eye" in the revision process is not just about making criticisms!

Recent upgrades in word-processing programs may also facilitate revisions in such a cooperative peer-revision process. Usually called a "track changes" feature, the programs permit several people to read each document file and make suggested deletions, insertions, and comments—each using separate distinctive colors for their recommendations. Thus, as the author, you may come back to your essay with a variety of suggestions and editorial comments. Most such programs then allow you to accept or reject each of those changes and incorporate your decisions about them into your final

---

2 Jeff Jeske, "Peer-Editing," in *Writing at Guilford: An Online Manual*, <http://www.guilford.edu/original/writing_manual/>, last modified 15 May 2001 [accessed 21 April 2001].

document. This sort of collaborative writing and revision process does take some getting used to, but has the advantage of easily consolidating comments and making it relatively easy to incorporate them into your final draft. It is a useful writing innovation which we think you would do well to explore.

For most writers, the process of improving drafts goes on until the last minute. Writing and revising drafts will help you focus on all parts of your work more clearly. It will help you see your thinking, your research, your factual knowledge, your expression, and the shape of your ideas. Very often as you write and rewrite drafts of your essay, you will realize that your thought is flabby, or you may suddenly think of contrary arguments you have not thought of before. You can then revise to take these contrary arguments into account. Reading your work over and over again, and taking advantage of comments from others, will help you track your own ideas. Once you have done so, you might better ensure they flow from one to another without leaving gaps that might hinder readers from making the connections you want them to make.

SUGGESTIONS ABOUT STYLE

■ ■ ■

Style in writing varies from writer to writer, and general agreement on style is hard to come by. Some historians are vivid and dramatic. Others are content to be more prosaic. Substance is always to be prized over surface in writing history. A beautiful writing style that conveys falsehood does nobody any good. But historians should remember a moral obligation to share their findings with the general public. Knowledge of history is a necessity of democratic government just because so many politicians appeal to history to justify their course of action. "History proves that we must do this or that," they say. Sometimes the best thing a historian can say is this: "History proves no such thing." Such a historian might have had a profound influence on Lyndon Johnson's determination not to be the first president who lost a war. Someone should have pointed out to him the American defeat in Canada in 1812. But then the historian must communicate the reasons for this judgment so readers can understand them.

The best advice is to write clearly enough so readers can understand your work without having you there to explain it to them. Most writers work hard all of their lives to develop a style they find both natural and attractive, one that others can understand and enjoy. No writer can please everybody. Shape your own style by making it as readable as you can, trying at the same time to avoid monotony of expression. A good style combines readability and variety without going so far as a variety that is ostentatious.

A brief chapter cannot tell you everything you need to know about style. But since beginning writers often lack confidence in their own writing, a few principles drawn from research on readability and the common practice of many mature writers may help. The following suggestions are meant as guides to the perplexed.

1. Write in coherent paragraphs.

Paragraphs are groups of sentences bound together by a controlling idea. You have been reading paragraphs throughout this book, taking them for granted because they are common to nearly all prose. Paragraphs help readability. Indentations break the monotony of long columns of type. They help readers follow the text with greater ease, providing special help when we lift our eyes from the page and must find our place again. They signal a slight change in subject from what has gone before. They announce that the paragraph to follow will develop a thought that can usually be summarized in a simple statement. The paragraph was not defined until the second half of the nineteenth century. Those who did the defining could not agree on how long a paragraph should be. The disagreement persists today. Long paragraphs can become disorganized. Even a well organized long paragraph may create eye strain. Short paragraphs may give an appearance of choppiness, of shifting from subject to subject without giving readers time to adjust. A good rule of thumb is to have one or two indentations on every typed manuscript page. It is only a rule of thumb—not a divine command. And it is a good idea to avoid the one-sentence paragraph common in journalism.

A lot of nonsense has been written about paragraphs in textbooks. The textbooks tell us that paragraphs have "topic sentences" and that the topic sentence may appear at the beginning, the middle, or the end. But the topic sentence is a myth. All paragraphs are built on the first sentence. It gives the direction that the paragraph should take, and the succeeding sentences in the paragraph should run in a natural flow from it.

Here is a paragraph by William Manchester, who in this part of a book on recent American history describes various political figures who became popular immediately after World War II. Manchester tells of Joseph McCarthy, who was elected to the U.S. Senate after World War II and became notorious for declaring that the federal government was infested with Communists. He never exposed a Communist, but he damaged many reputations before he was censured by the Senate in 1954 for irresponsible character assassination. He drank himself to death in 1957.

> Joe McCarthy, late of the Marine Corps, was reelected circuit judge in 1945. He immediately began laying plans to stump his state in the following year under the slogan, "Wisconsin Needs a Tail Gunner in the Senate," telling voters of the hell he had gone through in the Pacific. In reality McCarthy's war had been chairborne. As intelligence officer for Scout Bombing Squadron 235, he had sat at a desk interviewing fliers who had returned from missions. His only wartime injury, a broken leg, was incurred when he fell down a ladder during a party on a seaplane tender. Home now, he was telling crowds of harrowing nights in trenches and dugouts writing letters to the families of boys who had been slain in battle under his leadership, vowing that he would keep faith with the fallen martyrs by cleaning up the political mess at home— the mess that had made "my boys" feel "sick at heart." Sometimes he limped on the leg he broke. Sometimes he forgot and limped on the other leg.[1]

The first sentence of this paragraph, *Joe McCarthy, late of the Marine Corps, was reelected circuit judge in 1945*, sets the topic. The second sentence picks up the main thought of the first sentence by using the pronoun *he* and by telling us something else about McCarthy. The third sentence continues the subject by telling us about *McCarthy's war*—and so through the paragraph. We could summarize this paragraph by saying, "Here is a collection of facts about the political rise of Joseph McCarthy after World War II."

---

[1] William Manchester, *The Glory and the Dream* (Boston: Little, Brown, 1973), 394.

In any good paragraph you can draw lines between connectors, words like the pronoun *he* in the paragraph about McCarthy, a pronoun repeated throughout the paragraph. Sometimes the connector will be a word in one sentence that is repeated in the next. The connectors tie your sentences together—and therefore link your thoughts. They keep your ideas and information in an orderly framework. You can often test paragraph coherence by seeing if every sentence has a connector word that joins its thought in some way to the previous sentence all the way back to the first sentence in the paragraph.

The structure of paragraphs is usually either serial or listing. In the *serial* pattern of paragraph development, the second sentence develops a word or thought in the first sentence, the third sentence develops a word or thought in the second sentence, the fourth sentence will develop a word or thought in the third sentence, and so on until the end. In the *list* pattern, sentences in the paragraph make a more or less interchangeable list of items that support the general statement made in the first sentence.

In the serial paragraph, the order of the sentences is difficult or impossible to rearrange because each sentence depends on the one immediately before it. In the list paragraph, the order can usually be rearranged after the first sentence because the sentences that come afterwards have an equal relation to that first sentence. The paragraph from William Manchester about Joe McCarthy is a typical serial paragraph. After the first sentence, each succeeding sentence rises naturally from the one before it. You cannot easily rearrange the sentences and preserve the meaning and the tone.

The following paragraph tells us some reasons why Ngo Dinh Diem, the dictator of South Vietnam in 1963, lost his position and his life. The first sentence makes a statement, and the later sentences support it, but they could be rearranged in a different order:

> Diem, though dedicated, was doomed by his inflexible pride and the unbridled ambitions of his family. Ruling like an ancient emperor, he could not deal effectively with either the mounting Communist threat to his

regime or the opposition of South Vietnam's turbulent factions alien-
ated by his autocracy. His generals—some greedy for power, others an-
tagonized by his style—turned against him. His end, after eight years in
office, came amid a tangle of intrigue and violence as improbable as the
most imaginative of melodramas.[2]

Stanley Karnow, the author of this paragraph, begins with
Diem's doom; Diem was assassinated. Having mentioned the
doom—foretold in earlier parts of his book—Karnow lists reasons
for it. He could just as easily have written the paragraph like this:

```
    Diem, though dedicated, was doomed by his
inflexible pride and the unbridled ambitions of his
family. His end, after eight years in office, came
amid a tangle of intrigue and violence as
improbable as the most imaginative of melodramas.
His generals—some greedy for power, others
antagonized by his style—turned against him. Ruling
like an ancient emperor, he could not deal
effectively with either the mounting Communist
threat to his regime or the opposition of South
Vietnam's turbulent factions alienated by his
autocracy.
```

All paragraphs do not fall as neatly into the two categories as
these. Writing is, thank heaven, not so simple. You may have a mix-
ture of serial sentences and listing sentences in the same paragraph.
But keeping in mind the distinction may help you make your own
writing more coherent.

In good paragraphs and essays (or chapters of books), patterns
of repetition hold all prose together. Pronouns, synonyms, and repeated nouns demonstrate that the writer is picking up thoughts
from earlier in the work and reasserting them to say more about
them. Our short-term memories require this kind of repetition so

---

[2] Stanley Karnow, *Vietnam: A History* (New York: Penguin Books, 1984), 277.

that as readers we are continually reminded of what has gone on before. Each sentence both repeats something from previous sentences—a word, a synonym, or an idea—and adds something new to the information we already possess.

Again, it is worth saying that the first sentence in the paragraph is normative for the rest of it. It sets both the subject and the tone for what follows, and all of the other sentences extend its meaning. Sometimes you can find something approximating the standard topic sentence of the English textbooks—a generalization that sums up everything in the paragraph—but often you cannot. Narrative paragraphs are likely to have nothing like the standard topic sentence. One thing happens after another in a series of sentences. Here is a narrative paragraph from Wallace Stegner's *The Gathering of Zion*, his story of the Mormon trail and the journey of Brigham Young's early group of Mormon immigrants to Utah. The "Revenue Cutter" is the name of a small boat the Mormons found operating on the river when they arrived at the crossing. Stegner calls the Mormons "saints" because that is what they called themselves:

> Travelers late in the season often found the North Platte here clear and shrunken and shallow enough to be waded. But in June it was a hundred yards wide and fifteen feet deep, with a current strong enough to roll a swimming horse. (It did in fact drown Myers' buffalo horse.) The Revenue Cutter could carry the wagons' loads, but the wagons themselves were a problem. While some of the saints brought down poles from the mountain and worked at making rafts, others experimented with swinging wagons across the river on a long rope tied to the opposite bank. Two wagons tied together keeled over on striking the far shore, breaking the reach of one and the bows of the other. Four lashed together proved to be stabler, but too heavy to handle. One alone, with an outrigger of poles to steady it, was caught by the current and the strong southwest wind and rolled over and over. The best system appeared to be ferrying one at a time on a clumsy raft. A backbreaking day of that, up to their armpits in icy water, and they had crossed only twenty-three wagons. It rained and hailed on them, and the wind blew. The river was rising so fast they were afraid of being held up for days; and thinking of themselves, they also thought of the great company crowded with women and children who would soon follow them.

Brigham put a crew to hewing two long dugout canoes from cottonwood logs and planking them over to make a solid ferryboat.[3]

The first sentence introduced the North Platte river, and the other sentences give in chronological order the events that took place as the Mormons set out to cross it. Nothing resembling the standard topic sentence is here to be found. Such a sentence is not necessary because the action builds sentence by sentence in a careful pattern of repetition that is clearly understandable. Although narrative paragraphs seldom have topic sentences, expository paragraphs may begin with a general statement developed in the paragraph itself. Expository paragraphs explain information. We explain documents or people or events by paying attention to details that make up a text, a personality, or a happening. We look at the relation of those details to one another. We try to understand what caused them and what they contribute to the whole. A general statement at the beginning of an analytical paragraph may express the idea that the paragraph will expand.

An article in a recent issue of the *American Historical Review* dealt with the development of shopping malls, or "shopping towns," as some people called them in the 1960s. Here is an analytical paragraph with a general statement that comes at the beginning. Victor Gruen was a developer in New Jersey at the time.

> While bringing many of the best qualities of urban life to the suburbs, these new "shopping towns," as Gruen called them, also sought to overcome the "anarchy and ugliness" characteristic of many American cities. A centrally owned and managed Garden State Plaza or Bergen Mall, it was argued, offered an alternative model to the inefficiencies, visual chaos, and provinciality of traditional downtown districts. A centralized administration made possible the perfect mix and "scientific" placement of stores, meeting customers' diverse needs and maximizing store owners' profits. Management kept control visually by standardizing all architectural and graphic design and politically by requiring all tenants to

---

[3] Wallace Stegner, *The Gathering of Zion* (New York: McGraw Hill, 1964), 148.

participate in the tenants' association. Common complaints of downtown shoppers were directly addressed: parking was plentiful, safety was ensured by hired security guards, delivery tunnels and loading courts kept truck traffic away from shoppers, canopied walks and air-conditioned stores made shopping comfortable year 'round, piped-in background music replaced the cacophony of the street. The preponderance of chains and franchises over local stores, required by big investors such as insurance companies, brought shoppers the latest national trends in products and merchandising techniques. B. Earl Puckett, Allied Stores' board chair, boasted that Paramus's model shopping centers were making it "one of the first preplanned major cities in America." What made this new market structure so unique and appealing to businessmen like Puckett was that it encouraged social innovation while maximizing profit.[4]

When you explain an idea or an event in history, you will help readers see where you are going if you present a generalization in the first sentence and develop this thought through the rest of the paragraph.

As we have said, the paragraph is a flexible form, and these suggestions about its structure are not rigid rules. But if you think of them when you write, you will develop greater coherence to your thought, and you can develop a feel for what should or should not be in a paragraph.

2. Illustrate major generalizations by specific references to evidence.

In our experience, students love the grand generalizations that seem to explain everything and to give to the student writer an air of authority. But generalizations are tricky business in writing history. The mysteries of the past are infinite and frustrating. We tire of the equivocations scholars make. "This may be true, but there is some evidence against it." "This may be false, but on the other hand, some evidence supports it." We want certainty, firmness, stern moral principles

---

[4] Lizabeth Cohen, "From Town Center to Shopping Center: The Reconfiguration of Community Marketplaces in Postwar America," *American Historical Review*, 101(October 1996): 1056.

that cannot be violated, and assurances of truth. And so it is easy for any of us to get caught up in some grand and definite generalization that seems to explain everything. Beware of that temptation!

Often we have had students, especially in survey courses, who launch grand generalizations like rockets aimed at the moon. "During Reconstruction Yankee carpetbaggers and Southern turn-coats called scalawags trampled the prostrate South into the dirt and so ravaged its economy that it could not recover for a century." "The Roman Empire fell because the Romans began to practice birth control and so reduced their population so much that the German tribes were able to make an easy conquest." "Germans are historically more aggressive and militaristic and more hostile to minorities than are the other people of Western Europe."

We have seen many such generalizations in student papers, and all of them make us want to reach for the Pepto-Bismol. None of them stands up under careful scrutiny of the evidence. In fact, the evidence makes these grand generalizations sound empty, even a bit foolish. It is easy to forgive young students for these enthusiasms of certainty, but the fact remains that history is endless careful discussion of the evidence, an edifice built brick by brick—and often remodeled while under construction. It is not a discipline that comes prefabricated so that all the history student has to do is take it out of the box and paste it together in a grand form that everybody agrees on before the box is opened.

One of the most important cautions for the budding historian is to avoid making the kind of sweeping generalization that makes readers lose confidence in your knowledge and your judgment. The best way to avoid the pitfalls of overgeneralization is to follow a simple rule: Provide supporting evidence for the generalization, and at the same time try to find any evidence that might seem to contradict your generalization. Be detailed enough in supporting your generalization, and fair enough in testing it so that your readers gain confidence that you know what you are talking about.

If you say that Woodrow Wilson had racist ideas, quote from his works to demonstrate them; search through his works for any evidence you can find that he was not a racist. Or if you contend that John L. O'Sullivan did not really invent the idea of Manifest Destiny, then use specific examples of previous references to bolster your contention, and explain how the term came to be used in the American past. The truth of history resides in the details. The details also give life to the past and make us see the connections between past and present. A related point is this: Make only the kind of generalization that you can readily support by details. Details can be quotations, statistics, summaries of events, and any number of other things. Study the paper on Manifest Destiny in Appendix A to see how Penny Sonnenburg supports her generalizations about the origins of the Manifest Destiny idea with quotations, summaries, and paraphrases of the sources.

3. To test the coherence of your papers, see if the first and last paragraphs have some obvious relations.

In most published writing, the first and last paragraphs of a book, a chapter in a book, or an article have such coherence that you can read them without reading the intervening material and have a fairly good idea of what comes between. Now and then you will find a piece of writing where the first and last paragraphs do not have a clear verbal connection. But writers wishing to be sure that their work holds together can help their efforts by seeing to it that each paper ends in a paragraph that reflects some words and thoughts appearing in the first. Notice how this is done in the sample paper in Appendix A.

Study articles in published journals to see for yourself how often this principle is observed in the professional writing of history. Turn through the pages of the *American Historical Review*, seeing first and last paragraphs mirroring each other. (Looking at first and last paragraphs is also a good way to see if the article includes information you may want to use in your own work.) You can also see that this mirroring of first and last paragraphs appears in popular journals of opinion such as *The Atlantic* or *The New Yorker.*

4. Keep sentences short enough to be manageable.

Sometimes writers lose control of their sentences and end with long, involved coils of words. Long sentences can be difficult. They slow readers down, hide your meaning, and make integration of that sentence to the sentences that come before it and after it difficult. Remember this cardinal rule: Every sentence in your essay picks up something from what has gone before and contributes something to what comes afterwards. To keep your own prose connected, you must strive always to keep this basic principle in mind.

Focus on the most important statement you want to make in every sentence. Don't entangle that statement with other information that you cannot develop or that is not a development of some previous information in your essay.

One way to keep sentences manageable is to avoid multiplying dependent clauses. Dependent clauses act as adjectives or adverbs and modify other elements in a sentence. They are necessary to writing. The most readable writing does not use a dependent clause in every sentence. A sentence may have one or two dependent clauses, but a couple of sentences that come after it may have no dependent clauses at all—like this paragraph from an article on the abnegation of French battlefield nurses in World War I. It is a dense but readable piece of prose:

> In the end the nurses' memoirs, like the commentaries, left intact the incongruity, even the opposition, of women and war. Targets of as much criticism as praise, nurses in their memoirs absolved themselves of the charge of pursuing feminine emancipation, solidarity, and values at the expense of masculine suffering by subordinating their wartime experience to the soldier's story. Rather than script a role for the volunteer nurse alongside the soldier in the War Myth, even the grimmest and most "realistic" of the nurses' memoirs placed the wounded soldier on a pedestal and the nurse, head bowed, at his feet, her emotional suffering a tribute to his sacrifice. In their personal accounts, France's nurse memoirists helped erase their own experiences from the public memory of the war. Their works did not reshape the War Myth to include women;

instead they commemorated World War I as the trench-fighters' war and confirmed the essence of the war experience as masculinity.[5]

We do not want to suggest you should avoid dependent clauses altogether, but to avoid making them so numerous that they cause you to lose control of your sentences and make your prose difficult to read. Don't write in the short, choppy sentences of a first-grade reader about Dick and Jane. But always ask yourself: Is this dependent clause necessary?

5. Begin most sentences with the subject.

Sentences are statements about subjects. In published American English, about three-fourths to four-fifths of the sentences and independent clauses within sentences begin with the subject. This principle is often undermined by well-meaning writing teachers who tell students to vary sentences by inverting them—that is, by putting the verb before the subject. Or they tell students to begin with a participle or to do something else to keep the subject from coming first. Yet any examination of published English in widely read books and articles will show the proportion of openings with the subject that we have mentioned here. Most sentences that do not begin with the subject will begin with some sort of adverb—a word, a phrase, or a clause that fulfills the common adverbial function of telling when, where, how often, or how much. Now and then a sentence begins with a participle or a participial phrase. You will help keep your thinking clear if in writing sentences you think first of the subject, then of what you want to say about it. Our natural way of composing sentences, whether we speak or write, is to name a subject and then to make a statement about it. Sometimes inexperienced writers are paralyzed by the thought that they begin too many sentences with the subject. They feel a laudable desire to vary their sentences by changing the beginnings. Sometimes the result is obscurity.

---

[5] Margaret H. Darrow, "French Volunteer Nursing and the Myth of War Experience in World War I," *American Historical Review,* 101(February 1996): 106.

This suggestion is more important than it may seem at first. Many sentences go astray and become hopelessly confused because writers don't know what they want to say. Be sure you write each sentence to make a clear statement about a subject. Don't bury your real subject in a dependent clause. Indeed, most readable writers use dependent clauses only once or twice in every three or four sentences. The main action of your sentence should be in the main clause. In that clause you should identify the subject as the element about which a statement is to be made.

6. Keep subjects as close to their verbs as possible.

The most readable writers seldom interrupt the natural flow of their sentences by placing a dependent clause after the subject. Like the general principle that most sentences begin with the subject, this is another one you can prove by reading almost any popular—and, therefore, readable—prose. It is not absolute. Every writer sometimes puts a word or a phrase or even a clause between a subject and a verb. But take care not to overdo it. Here is a fine, readable paragraph by historians Oscar and Lilian Handlin; note the close relation between subjects and verbs in this paragraph.

> The healing image meant much to a government, not all of whose statesmen were pure of heart and noble of impulse. On January 30, 1798, the House of Representatives being in session in Philadelphia, Mr. Rufus Griswold of Connecticut alluded to a story that Mr. Matthew Lyon of Vermont had been forced to wear a wooden sword for cowardice in the field. Thereupon Mr. Lyon spat in Mr. Griswold's face. Sometime later, Mr. Griswold went to Macalister's store on Chestnut Street and bought the biggest hickory stick available. He proceeded to the House, where, in the presence of the whole Congress and with Mr. Speaker urging him on, he beat Mr. Lyon about the head and shoulders. An effort to censure both actors in the drama failed.[6]

---

[6] Oscar and Lilian Handlin, *Liberty in Expansion: 1760–1850* (New York: Harper & Row, 1989), 160.

Making sure you connect the subjects of your sentences closely to the verbs which describe the actions they are taking will also help you focus on another important stylistic element of good writing.

7. Avoid the passive voice whenever possible.

In sentences using the passive voice, the verb acts on the subject. In the active voice, the subject acts through the verb. Here is a sentence in the active voice: *President John F. Kennedy made the decision to invade Cuba.* Here is a sentence in the passive voice: *The decision was made to invade Cuba.* You see at once a problem in the passive voice. It often hides the actor in the sentence. In the active voice we know who made the decision. In the passive voice we do not know who made the decision unless we add the somewhat clumsy prepositional phrase *by President John F. Kennedy.* Announcements by governments frequently use the passive voice. "Mistakes were made," says one government press release that we read not long ago. The passive shields us from knowing who made the mistakes.

Readable historians use the passive voice only when they have a reason for doing so. Use the passive when the obvious importance of the sentence is that the subject is acted upon: *Bill Clinton was elected to a second term as President of the United States in November 1996.* The passive may also help keep the focus of a paragraph on a person or group where the agent is understood throughout. In the following paragraph from Orlando Figes's history of the Russian Revolution of 1917 and afterward, the passive is used several times. Passive clauses are in italics. Study them to understand how the author uses the passive voice:

> The Kronstadt Naval Base, an island of sailor-militants in the Gulf of Finland just off Petrograd, *was by far the most rebellious stronghold of this Bolshevik vanguard.* The sailors were young trainees who had seen very little military activity during the war. They had spent the previous year cooped up on board their ships with their officers, who treated them with more than the usual sadistic brutality since the normal rules of naval discipline did not apply to trainees. *Each ship was a tinderbox*

of hatred and violence. During the February Days the sailors mutinied with awesome ferocity. *Admiral Viren, the Base Commander, was hacked to death with bayonets, and dozens of other officers were murdered, lynched or imprisoned in the island dungeons.* The old naval hierarchy was completely destroyed and effective power passed to the Kronstadt Soviet. It was an October in February. *The authority of the Provisional Government was never really established, nor was military order restored.* Kerensky, the Minister of Justice, proved utterly powerless in his repeated efforts to gain jurisdiction over the imprisoned officers, *despite rumours in the bourgeois press that they had been brutally tortured.*[7]

The focus of the paragraph is the consequence of the uprising of the sailors at Kronstadt. The passive helps to keep that focus.

Our best advice is this: When you use the passive voice, ask yourself why you are doing it. If you do not have a clear reason for the passive, put your sentence in the active voice.

8. Write about the past in the past tense.

Inexperienced writers striving for dramatic effect will often shift into the historical present. They may write something like this:

```
        The issue as Calvin Coolidge sees it is this:
The government has been intervening too much in
private affairs. He is now the head of the
government. He will do as little as possible. He
takes long naps in the afternoon. He keeps silent
when people ask him favors. He says things like
this: "The chief business of the American people is
business." He does not believe the government
should intervene in the business process. Within a
year after Coolidge leaves office, the Great
Depression begins.
```

The effort here is to provide life to the drama of history, to make it seem that it is all happening again as we read. Some students copy

---

[7] Orlando Figes, *A People's Tragedy: A History of the Russian Revolution* (New York: Viking, 1997), 394–395.

this form from what they hear on television, and in particular from sportscasters who have adopted such phrasing in an attempt to make their reports more exciting. But in American and British convention, it is most appropriate to use the past tense to write about the past. The present becomes tedious after a while—and often confusing.

It is, however, permissible to use the present tense in describing a piece of writing or a work of art, because such works are assumed to be always present to the person who reads it or observes it. Therefore, you can say something like this: "The Fourteenth Amendment to the Constitution gives to the citizens of the various states all the rights guaranteed under the Federal Constitution." Sometimes it may be better to use the past tense. This is especially true when you do not intend to give an extended summary of the work:

> In his "Cross of Gold" speech delivered at the Democratic National Convention in 1896, William Jennings Bryan took the side of the impoverished farmers who thought that inflation would help raise the prices they received for their crops.

In this case, the emphasis is on Bryan rather than on the speech itself; thus the simple past tense seems more appropriate.

9. Avoid overusing adjectives and adverbs.

Adjectives modify nouns; that is, they change the meaning of nouns somewhat. Adverbs modify verbs, adjectives, and other adverbs. Both adjectives and adverbs can weaken the words they modify. A good adjective or adverb, well used in a necessary place, can brighten a sentence. Sometimes inexperienced writers will use several adverbs or adjectives in a usually vain effort to paint a fuller and richer picture for their readers. But too many of them thicken and slow down the flow of prose. The best advice is to use both sparingly.

The proportion of one adjective to every 12 or 13 words is fairly constant among published writers in America. The proportion of adverbs to other words is somewhat less. Of course, these proportions are not absolute. For some purposes you may have to use more adjectives and adverbs than normal. Be sure you need the adjectives and adverbs you use. Sometimes there are other writing techniques which may accomplish similar goals and may, at the same time, add variety to your prose.

10. Use an occasional rhetorical question, metaphor, or simile to enliven your writing.

There are several writing techniques in the English language which, while not literal expressions, you likely will find helpful from time to time in your writing. Using them will add the sort of variety which characterizes much good writing. The rhetorical question is one that you, the writer, ask so that you may define a problem you wish to pursue. You ask the question to answer it yourself. Here is a rhetorical question placed near the beginning of an essay on concepts of honor in the American South before the Civil War.

> Sometimes white men of the antebellum South pulled or tweaked one another's noses. Slaves never pulled anyone's nose; neither did white women. Nose pulling was a meaningful act that appeared almost exclusively in the active "vocabulary" of white men. To pull a nose was to communicate a complex set of meanings to an antagonist and an audience. What did the act mean to the men who performed it and witnessed it?[8]

This rhetorical question opens to Professor Kenneth S. Greenberg ways of defining the concept of "honor" among Southern white men before the Civil War, and he has written a fascinating essay.

Metaphors and similes appeal to some familiar experience or perception to illustrate something less familiar. They, too, can help you communicate with your readers. Here is Civil War historian

---

[8] Kenneth S. Greenberg, "The Nose, the Lie, and the Duel in the Antebellum South," *American Historical Review,* 95 (February 1990): 57.

Shelby Foote, speaking of the danger sharpshooting snipers posed to troops in the line, even during lulls in the fighting:

> Because of them, rations and ammunition had to be lugged forward along shallow parallels that followed a roundabout zigzag course and wore a man down to feeling like some unholy cross between a pack mule and a snake.[9]

Such metaphors and similes enliven writing. Don't carry them to excess. Used discreetly, they can be a great help.

However, take care to avoid clichés, the tired old expressions that we have heard time and again. The essence of a cliché is its predictability. When we hear the beginning of the expression, we know what the end will be. We know that a bolt is always from the blue, although we seldom think that the person who speaks of the bolt from the blue is speaking of lightning striking on a clear day. We know that unpleasant facts are "cold, hard facts" and that the determining influence in a discussion is the "bottom line." These are expressions that require no thought on the part of the writer and that inspire no thoughts in the reader.

If you think about the stylistic devices suggested in this chapter, you may begin looking more closely at writing you enjoy. Look at the forms writers use to keep you moving through their words. Learning to read in this way is part of learning to write. You learn to read and write best not by consulting a book of grammar and syntax, but by noticing carefully the devices good writers use to woo readers.

Nonetheless, answering the questions on this summary checklist may also help you begin improving your writing and developing a distinct writing style of your own:

---

[9] Shelby Foote, *The Civil War: A Narrative*, vol. 3 (New York: Random House, 1974), 297.

Writer's Checklist

_____ ✔ Is each of my paragraphs a coherent whole?

_____ ✔ Are my generalizations supported by evidence?

_____ ✔ Do my first and last paragraphs have some obvious relationship?

_____ ✔ Have I kept my sentences short and manageable?

_____ ✔ Do most of my sentences begin with the subject?

_____ ✔ Are my subjects in close proximity to my verbs?

_____ ✔ Do I have clear reasons for the few times I use passive voice?

_____ ✔ Do I write about the past in the past tense?

_____ ✔ Have I been judicious in using adjectives and adverbs?

_____ ✔ Do I occasionally use a rhetorical question, metaphor, or simile?

7

WRITING CONVENTIONS

∎ ∎ ∎

Historians are a broad community. Like most communities, they have their conventions, their ways of doing things. The conventions are not laws. People are not arrested and put in jail for violating them. Even so, members of the community notice when conventions are violated—just as they notice when someone blows his nose on a linen table napkin at a formal dinner or spits on the floor in church. Social conventions are violated if, when you are introduced to a perfect stranger, you howl with laughter and tell him that he is the ugliest person you have ever seen—even if he is. All conventions change from age to age and region to region. Even as they change, communities depend on conventions and find them necessary. They help you know what to expect and have confidence in yourself in various situations. They are not logical; they are simply customary. People once shook right hands when they met to prove they did not conceal a weapon in their fist. Left-handers, consequently, developed a sinister reputation in the ancient world because they could shake right hands and conceal a weapon in the left. Today you may still put out your right hand, and so do most of the lefties you know, and nobody ever thinks of weapons. Shaking hands is now merely a convention, and to refuse to shake hands with someone may be seen as an insult.

If anything, the conventions of writers are more strict than social conventions. If you violate the conventions, you run the risk of not being taken seriously. Your readers may even turn hostile toward what you write because you seem to insult them by refusing to live up to their expectations. It makes no sense for a writer to irritate readers. It's hard enough to get them to pay attention to you without putting more obstacles in their way! For historians, the primary guide to writing conventions is the *Chicago Manual of Style*. We have followed that *Manual* in making the suggestions in this chapter as well as in Chapter 8, where we consider the conventions for documenting sources. Some of you may be more familiar with Kate L. Turabian, *A Manual for Writers of Term Papers, Theses, and Dissertations*, which is based almost entirely on the *Chicago Manual*. Of course, you should always check with your instructors about any particular suggestions or instructions they or your college may wish you to follow in addition to those that we mention below.

USING QUOTATIONS

You will frequently quote both from primary and secondary sources. These quotations (not "quotes") will give authority to your papers. There are some things about using quotations in your essays that you should remember. Perhaps most importantly, use quotations sparingly; resist any temptation to use even one-quarter as much quoted material as you would your own words. Always use quotations for particular reasons that will advance the argument in your essay. A writer who does so "is not a drone," as the respected American historian Jacques Barzun observed years ago; rather, "he has paid his fellows tribute by naming them in the text or in footnotes."[1] That being the case, a writer should take care to present quotations using the accepted conventions for doing so.

---

[1] Jacques Barzun, *On Writing, Editing, and Publishing*, 2nd ed. (Chicago: University of Chicago Press, 1986), 125–126.

1. It is nearly always better to use shorter quotations rather than longer ones.

It is not always necessary to use full sentence quotations. You can often incorporate a phrase or a clause from a source into your own sentences and give the flavor and the information you want to convey:

> Bruce Catton called the battle between the ironclad ships *Monitor* and *Merimack* a "strange fight," for, as he said, "Neither ship could really hurt the other."

2. Use the American style for quotation marks.

The primary American quotation mark is made with two apostrophes set together like this:

> "History is the essence of innumerable biographies," Thomas Carlyle said.

Quotations within quotations are set off with single apostrophes like this:

> Wilcox declared, "I entirely reject Carlyle's statement that 'History is the essence of innumerable biographies' because history is both more and less than biography."

3. Periods and commas used at the end of quotations always go within the quotation marks, while semicolons and colons always go outside the final quotation marks.

Study the following examples carefully:

> "We learn from history that we learn nothing from history," Hegel said.
>
> Voltaire said, "The history of the great events of this world is scarcely more than the history of crimes."

"He is yellow because he recklessly distorts Negro crimes, gives them a disproportionate place in life, and colors them dishonestly to inflame the ignorant and the credulous"; such was the judgment of Francis Hackett on the "yellow journalism" of the Reverend Thomas Dixon, author of the novel made into the movie *Birth of a Nation*.

4. A question mark at the end of a quotation goes within the final quotation marks only if the quotation itself is a question.

A question mark goes outside the final quotation marks if the quotation is not a question but is used within a question. Here is an example of a question mark that is part of the quotation:

> Professor Young posed this question: "Why was a blatantly racist movie such as *Birth of a Nation* so popular?"

And here is an example of a question mark that is not part of the quotation:

> What did Francis Hackett, writing of the Reverend Thomas Dixon in the March 20, 1915, *New Republic*, mean when he said, "So far as I can judge from this film, as well as from my recollection of Mr. Dixon's books, his is the sort of disposition that foments a great deal of the trouble in civilization"?

5. For any quotation longer than four or five lines, indent the entire quotation five spaces, and set it up as a block within your text.

Double-space the block quotation, and do not enclose it with quotation marks. Your instructor may want you to put block quotations in single-space text since your essays usually will not be for publication. Since it is difficult to edit single-spaced text, you would always double-space any material intended for publication.

While you do not put quotation marks around a block quotation, you should use quotation marks within the block quotation as they appear in the quoted source you are using.

6. Use ellipsis marks to indicate words you leave out between quotation marks.

In typing, you make ellipsis marks using three dots or periods, placing a space between each dot and whatever comes before and after it . . . like this. Word processing programs, however, frequently enter the three small dots automatically or as a single character, so they may appear...more like this. Here is an example of how ellipsis marks are used in presenting a quotation in your paper. The original source is this:

> The Rosenbergs were not, prior to their arrest, anyway, prominent national figures.

A quotation with some words left out indicated by ellipsis marks would appear like this:

> In his history of political murder, Franklin L. Ford says of the Rosenbergs, executed for spying in 1953, "The Rosenbergs were not . . . prominent national figures."

You should *not* use ellipsis marks at the beginning or end of a quotation. Some writers begin quotations with ellipsis marks to indicate that the quotation does not include all of a text. Remember, however, that the quotation marks themselves indicate that the quoted material is separated from its source. Use of ellipsis marks at the beginning or end of a quotation is redundant and annoying.

7. Change capital letters to lowercase, or lowercase letters to capitals, in quoted material when your purpose is to make the quotation fit into your own sentence.

Here is a sentence from Richard Ellmann's biography *James Joyce* where Ellmann comments on the city of Trieste in 1920 when, in consequence of World War I, it had passed from Austrian to Italian rule:

> Under Austria the city had been full of ships; now the harbor was almost deserted.

Here is one way to the use the quotation in writing an essay:

> Ellmann, writing of Joyce's return to Trieste in 1920, says that "under Austria the city had been full of ships; now its harbor was almost deserted."

Do not use brackets to indicate that you have changed the capitalization of the *U* in *under.* The brackets are unnecessary and distracting. In fact, this approach to using quotations by integrating them into your own prose can often give your essays an extra sparkle in the minds of your readers.

Whenever you decide to use quotations in your papers, keep these questions in your mind:

Writer's Checklist

- _____ ✔ Are the quotations I use shorter rather than longer?
- _____ ✔ Have I used the American style for quotation marks?
- _____ ✔ Have I placed punctuation outside or inside quotation marks appropriately?
- _____ ✔ Are block quotations set apart, without quotation marks?
- _____ ✔ Have I used ellipsis marks properly?
- _____ ✔ Are the quotations I use made to blend into *my* prose?
- _____ ✔ Have I quoted too often?

MECHANICS AND GRAMMAR

Most people feel anxious about grammar, supposing they do not know it well and imagining they make mistakes all the time. In fact, most of us know grammar well enough to use it appropriately much of the time. Written language is more formal than spoken language; writing is more difficult than speaking. Sometimes in the physical labor of writing, our minds wander, and we make errors. That is, we violate conventions. Most people can spot their errors in grammar by reading their work carefully aloud. You can usually trust your ear. When something doesn't sound right, check it out in an English handbook, or ask a friend. Writers collaborate all the time in real life; they should collaborate in school, too. As we suggested in Chapter 5, peer editing is a valuable way to work on revisions of your draft essays.

The grammar we use in writing is set by editors and writers themselves. It has not changed much in the last century. You encounter it in textbooks, magazines, daily newspapers, and your own writing. It is part of mass literacy—the general expectation in the modern world that most people can read. Mass production of any sort requires standardization and simplification of grammar. By following the conventions, you increase the ease with which readers follow your work.

The following are some sources of common difficulties. The list does not represent a complete summary of English grammar. If you discover other problems in your writing, get a good English language writing handbook and study areas that give you the most difficulty.

1. Make sure each of your sentences has a subject and verb and that they agree.

That is, be sure you write in complete sentences, and that plural verbs go with plural subjects and singular verbs go with singular subjects. Reading your draft aloud will call attention to some of these problems, but there are also other troublesome areas.

Difficulties can arise when you have a prepositional phrase with a plural object after a single subject. Rather than this:

His statement of grievances *were* read to the assembly.

Write this:

> His statement of grievances *was* read to the
> assembly.

Use singular verbs after indefinite pronouns such as *anybody, everybody, anyone, everyone, somebody, someone, either, neither,* and *none.*

> Everyone *was* ready.
> Neither *was* possible.

None is occasionally used with a plural verb, as in,

> None of the children were ready to leave the
> circus.

However, most writers still prefer to say,

> None of the advantages was as important as the
> sum of the disadvantages.

Some collective nouns and phrases give problems. More traditional writers still say, "The majority of her followers *was* not convinced." But some will say, "The majority of his followers *were*," seeing *majority* as a collective noun that can take a plural verb. The sky will not fall if you use either form.

The phrase *a number of* followed by a prepositional phrase with a plural noun always takes a plural verb:

> A number of the spectators were more
> interested in the fight than in the football game.

2. Take care to form the plurals of words accurately.

Always make the plural of nouns ending in *-est* and *-ist* by adding *-s* to the singular form. The plural of *guest* is *guests;* the plural of *scientist* is *scientists;* the plural of *humanist* is *humanists.*

Be sure to note differences between plurals and collective nouns. For example, the singular is *peasant,* the plural is *peasants,* but the collective class in European history is called the *peasantry.* We may call a man or woman who works in a factory a *proletarian,* and a group of them on an assembly line might be called by Marxists *proletarians.* But Marx called the whole class the *proletariat.* We may speak of a *noble* or an *aristocrat* when we speak of highest social ranks in some societies, and a group of such people would be called *nobles* or *aristocrats,* but the whole class is called the *nobility* or the *aristocracy.*

Take care not to use an apostrophe to form a plural. Do not write,

```
    The Wilsons' went to Washington.
```

The correct form is,

```
    The Wilsons went to Washington.
```

The plurals of dates and acronyms do not use the apostrophe: We speak of the 1960s or the NCOs (noncommissioned officers such as sergeants) in the armed forces.

3.   Form the possessive correctly.

The possessive shows ownership or a particular relation. We speak of *John's pen* or *Charlie's aunt.* Some writers and editors add only an apostrophe to singular nouns ending in *-s.* Thus we would have *Erasmus' works* or *Chambers' book.* But we believe the better practice is to make the possessive of these works as you would do others. Thus it would be *Erasmus's works* and *Chambers's book.*

For plural nouns that end in *-s,* add an apostrophe to form the possessive: *the Germans' plan;* or *the neighbors' opinions.* For plurals that do not end in *-s* form the possessive as you would for singular nouns: *women's history* or *children's rights.*

4. Make a distinction between common words that sound alike but are written differently.

For example, the contraction *it's* stands for *it is*, or, sometimes, *it has*. The possessive pronoun *its* stands for "belonging to it." Here are some examples of the appropriate usage:

> *It's* almost impossible to guarantee safe travel.
>
> *It's* been hard to measure the effects on the country.
>
> The idea had lost *its* power before 1900.

Similarly, you should distinguish appropriately between the contraction *you're*, meaning *you are*, the possessive *your*, and the noun *yore* occasionally used to describe the past. Each of these should be used as in the following examples:

> *You're* going to the picnic, aren't you?
>
> Will you take *your* umbrella?
>
> We will have a good time, just as in days of *yore*.

You will recognize that these distinctions are frequently ones which your computer's program for spell checking will not recognize, so they require you to be especially vigilant in proofreading your essay. Perhaps the most common such error that we see in student papers is the accidental confusion between plural possessive *their* and the noun or adverb *there*, specifying a particular place. Pay careful attention to this difference, as in the following sentence, so you will not leave the impression you are unaware of distinction.

> They put *their* picnic basket over *there*, next to the tree.

5. Use the objective case of pronouns correctly.

The nominative or subjective case of pronouns includes the forms *I, we, he, she, who, they,* and *those*. The objective case includes forms such as *me, us, him, her, whom,* and *them.* The nominative case is used as the subject of a sentence or a clause:

```
I read Huizinga's books
It was said that he was not the king's son.
```

The objective case should be used for the object of a preposition:

```
It was a matter between him and me.
Between you and me, I would say the policy was
wrong.
```

The objective case should be used in an indirect object:

```
The President gave her a Cabinet position.
```

The objective case should be used as the subject or an object of an infinitive verb. The infinitive is the verb form that includes the infinitive marker *to* and the dictionary form of the verb. Thus *to go, to be, to dwell,* and *to see* are all infinitives. The subject of the infinitive is a noun or pronoun that comes before the infinitive in a sentence, that does the action the infinitive expresses:

```
King Leopold wanted him to go at once to
Africa.
```

In the preceding example, the person designated by the objective pronoun *him* will go to Africa. Since he will do the going, the action expressed in the infinitive *to go,* the pronoun *him* is the subject of the infinitive and is in the objective case.

```
The prime minister supposed both Russell and
me to be damaged by the report.
```

In this example, the pronoun before the infinitive receives the action of the infinitive—here, an infinitive phrase.

**6. In clauses that begin with *who, whom, whoever,*
or *whomever,* the case of the pronoun is
determined by how it is used in the clause, not
how the clause is used in the sentence.**

Sometimes people eager to show that they know how to use
who or *whom* will use *whom* where *who* is the correct choice. The
problem is especially acute in the use of the word *whomever,* a vari-
ant of *whom.* Sometimes our students write sentences like this one:

> In the nineteenth century, women and children
> worked for *whomever* paid them pennies for a 14-hour
> day.

The fastidious writer of this sentence, knowing that the object of a
preposition takes the objective case, writes the preposition *for* and puts
whomever after it. But here, the entire clause is the object of the preposition. The pronoun should be *whoever* because it is the subject of the
clause. The pronoun is governed by how it is used in the clause, not by
how the clause is used in the sentence. So the sentence should read:

> In the nineteenth century, women and children
> worked for *whoever* paid them pennies for a 14-hour
> day.

The same principle applies in a common sentence form where
a parenthetical clause appears after the pronoun *who.* You should
not write this:

> The Indians *whom* Custer thought were only a
> small band in fact numbered in the thousands.

Rather, you should write this:

> The Indians *who* Custer thought were only a
> small band in fact numbered in the thousands.

The clause that determines the case of *who* is this:

```
who were only a small band
```

The words *Custer thought* are parenthetical.

7. Avoid confusion in making pronouns refer to antecedents.

Pronouns stand for nouns. Definite pronouns such as *he, she, it, him, her, they, them,* and *their* stand for nouns that usually appear somewhere before them in a sentence or paragraph. Be sure to make the pronoun reference clear even if you must revise the sentence considerably. Don't do this:

```
The Czechs disdained the Slovaks because they
were more cosmopolitan.
```

To whom does the pronoun *they* refer? Were the Czechs or the Slovaks more cosmopolitan? You must rewrite the sentence:

```
The more cosmopolitan Czechs disdained the
more rural Slovaks.
```

8. Be sure that participial phrases at the beginning of a sentence modify the grammatical subject.

You can make your prose incomprehensible and even ridiculous if you violate this widely accepted convention:

```
Living in a much less violent society, the
idea that every man, woman, and child in the United
States has a right to his or her very own assault
rifle seems ridiculous to most Canadians.
```

Who or what lives in that less violent society? The idea? The sentence should read like this:

```
Living in a much less violent society,
Canadians find ridiculous the idea that every man,
```

```
woman, and child in the United States has the right
to his or her very own assault rifle.
```

Avoid making an opening participle modify an expletive *it*. The expletive *it* is the pronoun without a referent and used as a subject: *It will rain.* The *It* does not refer to a previous noun. Avoid constructions like this:

```
        Steaming toward Europe, it seemed wise to him
to hide from photographers on the ship.
```

Instead write this:

```
        Steaming toward Europe, he tried to avoid
photographers on the ship.
```

9. Use commas carefully and appropriately, as in the following instances:

a) Commas set off independent clauses from one another. Independent clauses can usually stand by themselves as sentences:

```
        The McNary-Haugen bill would have provided
subsidies for American farmers, but President
Coolidge vetoed it in 1927.

        The people of the United States decided that
they must give up Prohibition, for warfare among
bootleggers was making the streets run with blood.
```

b) Use commas to set off long introductory phrases and clauses:

```
        Even after the transcontinental railroad was
completed in 1867, some pioneers still made the
trip west by covered wagon.
```

```
     After the American entry into the war of 1917,
the victory of the Allied Powers over the Germans
was assured.
```

c) Use commas to set off items in a series:

```
     President Franklin D. Roosevelt moved to solve
problems of unemployment, banking, and despair.
```

```
     William Jennings Bryan campaigned for the
presidency in 1896 by traveling 18,000 miles,
making 600 speeches, and attacking the "moneyed
interests."
```

d) Use commas to set off nonrestrictive clauses and phrases. You can remove the nonrestrictive clause and still have an intelligible sentence:

```
     Henry David Thoreau, one of the greatest
American writers, died of tuberculosis.
```

Do not use commas to set off restrictive clauses—clauses necessary if the main statement of the sentence is to be correctly understood:

```
     The man who robbed the bank on one day came
back the next and stole all of the calendars.
```

e) Commas separate two or more adjectives before a noun when you can substitute the word *and* for the comma and still have a sensible sentence:

```
     Ralph Waldo Emerson was a tall, frail, and
elegant man.
```

(You could say, "Ralph Waldo Emerson was a tall and frail and elegant man.") Do not use commas between adjectives where you cannot sensibly replace the comma with *and*. You can say,

```
     The three old maple trees stood on the hill.
```

But you cannot say,

> ```
> The three and old and maple trees stood on
> the hill.
> ```

f) Be sure that clauses acting as adjectives clearly modify the noun they are intended to modify in the sentence. Modification is usually clearest when the modifying clause comes immediately after the noun it modifies. Often confusions in modification result when a writer puts too much in one sentence. Avoid writing this:

> ```
> Japanese bankers in the nineteenth century
> thought that learning Chinese was necessary to
> doing business in the interior of China, which
> English bankers rejected.
> ```

In reading this sentence rapidly (as we read most things), we are suddenly struck by confusion. What did English bankers reject? Doing business in the interior of China? China itself? The interior of China? The sentence needs to be recast:

> ```
> Japanese bankers in the nineteenth century
> thought that learning Chinese was necessary to
> doing business in the interior of China, but
> British bankers thought the Chinese should learn
> English.
> ```

Sometimes the problem arises when writers follow the admirable policy of keeping subject and verb close together, but they then decide to tack an adjectival clause on the end of the sentence, and so cause confusion:

> ```
> The Dreyfus Case weakened confidence in the
> French Army which unleashed furious passions in the
> French public.
> ```

The writer meant to say this:

> The Dreyfus Case unleashed furious passions in the French public and weakened confidence in the French army.

g) Do not join independent clauses with commas alone. Don't write this:

> The Fugitive Slave Act required free states to return escaped slaves to their owners in the South, in effect it removed the limits of safety for fleeing slaves from the Ohio River to the Canadian border.

You could put a period after the word *South* and begin a new sentence with *In effect,* or you can replace the comma with a semicolon and leave the sentence otherwise as it is.

10. Don't break the parallel form of a series.

English and American writers often use words or phrases in a series, frequently in units of three. We speak of exorcising a demon in the Middle Ages "by bell, book, and candle." We write sentences like this:

> The moral principle of seeking the greatest good for the greatest number motivated Rousseau, Bentham, and Mill.

The units in the series must stand as grammatical equals. Therefore, you should not write sentences like this:

> Richelieu wanted three things for France: authority for the king, an end to religious strife, and he also wanted secure 'natural' frontiers.

The first two elements of this faulty series are nouns modified by prepositional phrases, but the last element is a clause. The sentence should be rewritten like this:

> Richelieu wanted three things for France:
> authority for the king, an end to religious strife,
> and secure 'natural' frontiers.

Use this checklist to help yourself polish some potential rough spots in your writing:

Writer's Checklist

_____ ✔ Have I written in complete sentences?

_____ ✔ Are my plurals formed correctly?

_____ ✔ Have I formed possessives accurately?

_____ ✔ Do I distinguish between words that sound alike but are written differently?

_____ ✔ Are my pronoun subjects and objects in the right form?

_____ ✔ Do my pronouns and participial phrases clearly refer to their subjects?

_____ ✔ Have I taken care to use commas appropriately?

_____ ✔ Have I kept the parallelism in my series statements?

THE FINAL MANUSCRIPT

The appearance of a manuscript tells readers many things about the writer. For one thing, they can tell what the writer thinks of them. A slovenly, scarcely legible manuscript is a sign that the writer cares little for the subject or the readers. The writer may care deeply—just as the parent who screams at children may love them. Still, it is not pleasant for children to be screamed at, and it is not pleasant for readers to be forced to read an almost illegible paper.

Computers make things easier for writers and readers alike, and most writers and students nowadays use computers with word-processing programs. Take advantage of the ability of the computer to generate clean copy. You can set the format of a computer to fit any manuscript style required by your instructor. As we suggested in Chapter 5, you can mark up a printed copy of your draft essay, then write the corrections in your word-processing program, save it to your disk, and print out a clean copy.

But keep in mind that formats for papers vary. Your teacher may give you a format to follow. Lacking instructions, you will not go wrong if you follow the format of the model research paper in Appendix A of this book. Here are some generally accepted conventions for the final presentation of your essay in manuscript form.

1. Use good quality 8½ × 11-inch white bond paper.

Some instructors prefer twenty-pound bond; it is heavy enough to handle easily and to make a nice contrast with the type or ink you use. Hard-pressed instructors reading three dozen research papers appreciate such favors. Do not turn in your final draft on flimsy or colored paper.

2. Print or type on one side of the page only.

Leave margins wide enough for comments your instructor may wish to make. Always double-space. Be sure the ink from the printer is dark enough to be read easily. Avoid using a tacky, hard-to-read font. Use Times New Roman, Bookman Old Style, Courier, or some other clean, easy-to-read type font in a standard size, usually 12 point. If your instructor will accept a handwritten paper, use lined white paper, and write in dark blue or black ink on every line. Do *not* use red, green, purple, or brown ink. Besides looking tacky, such inks tire your reader's eyes.

3. Use a cover page for your papers.

On it place the title, your name, the name of your instructor, the name of your course, and the time your class meets. Teachers who grade many papers sometimes get them mixed up on their desks. You will help your hardworking teacher immeasurably if you make it easy for him or her to place your work. The title page is not numbered, although it is counted as page 1, and the title itself should not be placed in quotation marks.

4. Number your pages.

When you do not number pages, you make your paper difficult to comment on and almost impossible to discuss in class. Sometimes teachers photocopy papers to distribute to the class for discussion. Sometimes papers even fall on the floor, and pages are scattered. Numbering pages is one of the basic conventions of writing that have been around since we stopped using scrolls. Every word-processing program numbers pages. Don't be lazy. Find the steps your program uses to number pages, and number them. Be professional.

5. Fasten the pages of your paper with a paper clip or with a staple in the upper left-hand corner.

Binders are almost always a nuisance to the instructor, adding bulk and making it awkward to write comments in the margins. It seldom is helpful to use them. We have colleagues who actually remove binders from student papers and throw them away.

6. Always make a second copy of your paper.

You may print two copies, or make a second with a photocopy machine. Papers do get lost. Computers break down. You may make mistakes on the keyboard and erase your work. Always make a second copy in case something happens to the original. If you use a computer, always make at least one backup disk with your essay on it.

7. Revise your paper enough to catch most casual errors.

As we have suggested previously, you should take care to eliminate typos, misspellings, words left out, words duplicated, and so on. Even so, you may find other mistakes just as you are ready to hand in the paper. You may even want to revise slightly at the last minute. Carefully write these corrections in black ink. Be sure your changes are neat and legible.

The presentation of your paper calls to mind the presentation of food in an expensive restaurant. You would not tip a waiter who served the main course on a plate he snatched out of a pile of dirty dishes, wiped off with his sleeve, and banged down on the table in front of you before he filled it with a dipper from a bucket that had a mop in it. You would stalk out of the place in anger. Your hardworking instructor, however, cannot stalk away from your sloppy paper. But if you ignore the conventions, you may discover that the grade is less than you desire.

Documenting Sources

■ ■ ■

When you write about history—or any other topic that requires research—you must use documentation that will allow your readers to check your sources. You know by now that historians depend on primary and secondary sources as they produce their stories of the past, that indeed to write history is always to write about sources. Other historians want to be able to check the evidence to see if the writer has cited it accurately and interpreted it soundly. Historians also use the documentation in books and articles they read to help them in their own research.

When you quote from a source or use information gathered from a source, tell your readers where to find the quotation or the information. When you quote the exact words of a source, enclose those words in quotation marks or use a block quotation to let readers know where you found them. If you summarize or paraphrase a source, let readers know what you are doing. Otherwise you may be guilty of plagiarism, and remember always that plagiarism is the writer's unpardonable sin. In the typical history paper, you will have many more notes acknowledging the source of ideas and paraphrased information than direct quotations.

BASIC PRINCIPLES

Here are some basic principles to help you know when to acknowledge that you have taken information from a source and what to include in your documentation.

1. Use a citation—a footnote, an endnote, or a mention in your text—whenever you quote directly from a source.

A good rule of thumb is to provide the source of any quotation of three or more successive words. Use quotation marks or a block quotation format (as we described in Chapter 7) to show that you are quoting. Here is a text from a secondary source, Frederick Pottle's *James Boswell: The Earlier Years 1740–1769*. He writes of Samuel Johnson, author of the first great English dictionary:

> Johnson was at this time in his fifty-fourth year, a huge, slovenly, near-sighted scholar, his face scarred by scrofula, his body distorted by compulsive tics, his speech interspersed with absent-minded clucks and mutterings.[1]

You might cite part of this text with a direct quotation followed by a footnote:

> When Boswell met him, Johnson was fifty-four years old, "a huge, slovenly, near-sighted scholar, his face scarred by scrofula, his body distorted by compulsive tics, his speech interspersed with absentminded clucks and mutterings."[1]

Or you can attribute your source within your own text like this:

> Frederick A. Pottle says that when Boswell met him, Johnson was fifty-four years old, "a huge, slovenly, near-sighted scholar, his face scarred by scrofula, his body distorted by compulsive tics, his speech interspersed with absent-minded clucks and mutterings."[1]

---

[1] Frederick A. Pottle, *James Boswell: The Earlier Years 1740–1769* (New York: McGraw-Hill, 1985), 113.

On occasion your instructor may ask you to write a short paper without footnotes or endnotes—perhaps a brief report, a position paper, a summary of your knowledge on a topic. Even without footnotes and endnotes, you can—and should—show in your text that you are quoting someone else's work. You can write, "According to Frederick A. Pottle . . ." or you can say, "Caroline Walker Bynum thinks that . . ."

2. Acknowledge any paraphrase or summary you make of someone else's thoughts.

Here is a paragraph from *The Hour of Our Death*, by Phillippe Ariès, a history of attitudes toward death in the Western world. Ariès writes about the denial of death in the nineteenth century, when people took a sentimental attitude toward death:

> Since death is not the end of the loved one, however bitter the grief of the survivor, death is neither ugly nor fearful. On the contrary, death is beautiful, as the dead body is beautiful. Presence at the deathbed in the nineteenth century is more than a customary participation in a social ritual; it is an opportunity to witness a spectacle that is both comforting and exalting. A visit to the house in which someone has died is a little like a visit to a museum. How beautiful he is! In the bedrooms of the most ordinary middle-class Western homes, death has come to coincide with beauty. This is the final stage in an evolution that began very quietly with the beautiful recumbent figures of the Renaissance and continued in the aestheticism of the baroque. But this apotheosis should not blind us to the contradiction it contains, for this death is no longer death; it is an illusion of Art. Death has started to hide. In spite of the apparent publicity that surrounds it in mourning, at the cemetery, in life as well as in art and literature, death is concealing itself under the mask of beauty.[2]

Here is a way to summarize this passage. The summary would require a formal citation to the source:

```
        Philippe Ariès tells us that in the
    sentimental nineteenth century, the terror of death
```

---

[2] Phillippe Ariès, *The Hour of Our Death*, trans. Helen Weaver (New York: Vintage Books, 1982), 473.

> was hidden under a cult of the beautiful. People
> gathered at the deathbed as if to share an exalting
> occasion, and after death the corpse was admired
> for its beauty. Such rituals were ways of hiding
> death by covering it with illusions. The thought
> seemed to be that if people could put a beautiful
> mask on death, it would cease to seem so horrible.[2]

The ideas here clearly come from the book by Ariès, even though they do not directly quote him. The author *must* make a citation to Ariès's work, saying, in effect, "This is where I got these ideas." As we said before, this kind of citation will usually be much more common in your papers than one documenting a direct quotation. That is, you will paraphrase or summarize much more frequently than you quote directly.

Ideas remain in some sense the property of the people who shape them and convey them to the world. You would never dream of writing about Sir Isaac Newton's laws of motion or Albert Einstein's theory of relativity as if you had discovered these ideas on your own! In much the same way, ideas about past events belong to the thinkers who conceived them, and you must acknowledge them when you use them in your own work. For example, the ideas of Phillippe Ariès on nineteenth-century sentimental attitudes about death may be helpful in understanding the enormous popularity of Tennyson's poem "Crossing the Bar," written in the nineteenth century. Were you to write a paper on Tennyson and his poem and employ Ariès ideas, you should certainly give Ariès credit, even if you do not quote him word for word in your own essay.

You do not, however, have to give sources for common knowledge, readily available in many sources, unless you quote directly from one of those sources. Nor do you need a citation for common expressions which have passed into general usage. You don't have to tell people that the sentence, "Pride goeth before destruction" comes from the Bible or that, "To be or not to be" comes from Shakespeare's *Hamlet*. If you are not sure whether some piece of information or an idea is common knowledge, ask your instructor or a reference librarian for an opinion.

3. Use forms of citations that allow readers to find your sources easily.

Read Penny Sonnenburg's essay on Manifest Destiny in Appendix A. Notice the forms of citations she uses. Although some of her sources are mentioned in the text, for the most part she uses footnote citations in her essay. They could just as well have been placed at the end of the paper as endnotes. Some institutions and individual teachers, as well as book and journal publishers, prefer one over the other for a variety of reasons. But from the writer's perspective, modern word-processing programs make easy the formatting and placement of either footnotes or endnotes as well as the capacity to change from one to the other almost at will. If you are unsure which to use, ask your instructor. In our own experience, both as students and faculty members, most instructors simply ask students to be consistent.

A number of style manuals also provide suggestions for forms of citations, including footnotes and endnotes; English handbooks used in freshman composition courses always have sections on writing research papers and include guidance on documentation of sources. The most comprehensive and authoritative manual for style and mechanics in many fields of study, including history, is *The Chicago Manual of Style*.[3] Generations of students have also used Kate L. Turabian, *A Manual for Writers of Term Papers, Theses, and Dissertations*,[4] a conveniently sized paperback condensation of the hefty *Chicago Manual of Style*. In addition to suggestions about stylistic conventions, both provide details for note citations and bibliographies (and also for parenthetical citations and associated reference lists, frequently used in the social sciences). Because the format of

---

[3] *The Chicago Manual of Style*, 14th ed. (Chicago: University of Chicago Press, 1993). This work is regularly updated, so you should be watchful for a new edition.

[4] Kate L. Turabian, *A Manual for Writers of Term Papers, Theses, and Dissertations*, 6th ed., rev. by John Grossman and Alice Bennett (Chicago: University of Chicago Press, 1996). As with the *Chicago Manual*, you should keep watch for a new edition.

note citations and bibliographies outlined in Turabian's book are the most widely used by historians, we have adopted that style for this book. Unless you receive specific instructions to the contrary, we urge you to do the same.

Whatever the style you are expected to use, it must lead readers to the precise location of material that is quoted or summarized in your paper. This requires that you pay particular attention to a number of details and make certain that they are presented carefully and consistently in your citations.

4. Make certain that the essential details are presented in the first citation to a particular source.

As we mentioned in Chapter 5, you need to take note of four essential elements about each of your sources. These same four elements also constitute the basis of the citations you will make in your paper. The first of these is *authorship*. Who created the work in question? When you think of this, be sure you also think about the names of editors and translators in addition to authors. Some works may have an editor and/or a translator in addition to the main author; a very few sources may have several individuals who contributed to the creation and presentation of the work. Their names will be indicated prominently, such as on the title page of books.

The second basic element is the *title*. What is the source called? The title of an article appearing as a separate part of a book or in a journal should be placed in quotation marks. The complete title of a book should be in italics if you use a word processor, or if you use a typewriter, the title should be underlined. Similarly, the title of a periodical—a scholarly journal, magazine, or newspaper—should be in italics (or underlined). While italics are also used for motion pictures and plays, use quotation marks for short poems or speeches which have titles. A few types of sources—such as some manuscripts—are merely described in regular type.

Since a major purpose for the citation is that others may find the same work, the third important element in your citation should be the *location* where you found the information. For books, this means place of publication and the publisher. For journals, you will need to list the volume (and sometimes the issue) number(s). In either case, pages numbers are also essential. Sometimes web sites and other electronic sources of information do not have discrete page numbers. In such cases you need to use a complete URL which will take a reader closest to the information you have found. And for manuscripts you will need to indicate both the collection name and the repository where they may be found.

The final element for your citation concerns the *date(s)* for your source. In the case of books, it is the year of publication; for journals, it is the year (and perhaps the month) of publication in addition to the volume number. Newspapers usually only have the date and not volume and issue numbers. For websites, the date they were created or last modified needs also to be included. Many high quality, reputable websites have such information clearly visible on the opening page of the site; in other cases, you may need to view the source information from your web browser to determine these dates. If no such dates are available, you should indicate *n.d.* for no date. Given concerns about the impermanence of URLs (and indeed of web sites themselves), many scholars suggest you also include the date you accessed the material on the web, including that within square brackets as you would for any information which you have supplied.

5. Use shortened forms of references in making subsequent citations to the same source.

When we first began our careers as historians, writers commonly used Latin abbreviations to make subsequent citations to sources they had already identified. This habit has gradually disappeared in academic writing. In their most recent editions, both the *Chicago Manual of Style* and Turabian's condensed guide recommend against using most of these. Both however, still suggest it may be appropriate in limited cases to use ibid. (for the Latin *ibidem*, "in the same place"). However, the increasing use of word-processing programs that allow for the easy movement of text—and the associated notes—from one location in an essay to another makes even that problematic. All too often we have found that notes transferred from one location in an essay to another cannot easily be associated with their previous referents, even for the authors. Thus we recommend the exclusive use of shortened forms for subsequent citations.

Often called "short author/short title" forms, such references can be both easily managed by authors and easily recognized by readers. In creating such shortened references, you should use the author's (or authors') surnames; you may, however, eliminate the names of translators and/or editors from subsequent references. If you use only one work from the same author(s) in your essay, then simply indicate the appropriate page and volume numbers in any subsequent citations. If you use more than one source from the same author, you will need to use a shortened title as well. However, for titles of four or five words, you can merely eliminate any initial article (*a, an,* or *the*) and use the entire title. In these cases, too, you will need to include appropriate volume and page references.

Use the following checklist to be sure you have followed the basic principles in documenting your sources. Then compare your citations to the sample suggestions in the remaining sections of this chapter to be certain you have made them clear to your readers.

Writer's Checklist

_____ ✔ Have I used a citation for every quotation in my essay?

_____ ✔ Are there clear citations to the sources of ideas I have taken from the works of others?

_____ ✔ Do all my citations explicitly identify all of the authors of my sources?

_____ ✔ Are the titles of all sources indicated in my citations?

_____ ✔ Have I made clear the locations where I found each of my sources?

_____ ✔ Do I indicate appropriate dates for each source citation?

_____ ✔ Can readers use my subsequent citations to identify the materials I have used?

ELECTRONIC SOURCES

In recent years, historians have become more concerned about the proliferation of both primary and secondary source materials available in electronic formats. In some cases these are merely digitized versions of printed (or, in a few cases, handwritten) materials. Along with most historians, we would recommend that when you have a choice and may use either a printed or an electronic version of a source, you opt for the printed version. Not least, the problems you face in making a citation to that source will usually be easier if you do so. But, as we have suggested in Chapter 4, there are many source materials that you will only be able to use in electronic formats. Therefore it is essential that you learn to make full and complete citations to such materials in your papers.

We have been concerned about the problem of electronic sources for some time. In fact, one of us created "A Brief Citation Guide for Internet Sources in History and the Humanities." You may wish to consult it at <http://www2.h-net.msu.edu/about/citation/>. However, since the Internet is an evolving institution, this guide probably cannot be considered definitive. And there are other types of electronic sources for which you may also need citation advice. So we also recommend that you also look at the more comprehensive and more regularly updated suggestions of Maurice Crouse, found at <http://www.people.Memphis.ed/~mcrouse/elcite.html>. Both of these are based upon the foundations laid out in the *Chicago Manual of Style* and condensed by Turabian, current editions of which are disappointing in reference to electronic materials. We have found that other electronic citation guides frequently are either based on other style manuals less familiar in historical writing or on principles which address electronic technology issues more than concerns of historical writing. So we urge you to use the H-Net and/or the Crouse guides in citing electronic sources in your history essays.

As we mentioned above, the Internet does pose special problems for those who want to make fixed references to documents that are frequently less than permanent and generally subject to alteration. Yet historians and humanists have for generations faced similar problems in citing sources. Private correspondence kept by families of its recipients or in duplicate copies made by the authors, for example, has long posed citation difficulties similar in nature to individual e-mail correspondence or, for that matter, materials in World Wide Web sites as well. And disappearing sources—such as long-out-of-print books apparently not saved in any repository or libray and archives destroyed by fire—have also been of concern to writers who used such materials but whose readers may not be able to locate them.

No method of citation can overcome these particular problems which, instead, cry out for great foresight in planning web sites and for careful explanations and web links to materials which may be moved. Still, such problems are real. Both of us have had our e-mail addresses change on several occasions as information technology departments at our universities have made upgrades in the electronic mail systems we use. While historians should be concerned about such problems and make efforts to seek solutions, as a writer you cannot solve them. So move forward, keep the basic principles we have outlined in mind, and make your citations as clear and complete as you can.

There are certain conventions in the use of the Internet that writers of history should follow. It is most appropriate, for example, to recognize the convention of angle (or pointed) brackets, < >, to enclose electronic addresses, either URLs or e-mail addresses. Some word-processing programs may automatically convert these to hyperlinks on your screen, on the assumption that you are only interested in electronic versions of your essays. Since many of you will be preparing printed versions, we suggest you remove the hyperlinks. To do so, move your cursor onto the link using the arrow keys on your keyboard. (You cannot use a mouse click to do this, however, since that will only activate the hyperlink!) Once the cursor is in place, you may use your word-processing program functions to remove the hyperlink. Then you can add (again, if necessary) the angle brackets before you print your essay.

Standard Internet practice is also to put the address on one line so that, if a hypertext link to that address is created within the document, it can be easily and accurately read and the electronic link to that site made seamlessly. An address which continues onto a second line often cannot be read as a complete address. But in printed citations it is often preferable for the address to continue from one line to another. When that is necessary, the compromise we suggest is that punctuation marks in Internet addresses (such as @ or . or / but not ~) be at the end of one line with only letters, numbers, or ~ beginning on the next line. (You need to be sure to remove any hyperlinks, too!)

Even this suggestion will not solve the problem of the URLs which are generated when you use some search engines. Often the resulting electronic addresses are at best unmanageable in citations and occasionally may not even be used as hyperlinks allowing readers to reach the same site. For example, using the search utility on the main H-Net website to locate the first electronic citation guide we listed above would result in finding messages in the H-Net logs containing that guide. One of these messages is identified by this URL: <http://h-net.msu.edu/cgi-bin/logbrowse.pl?trx=vx&list=h-africa&month=9602&week=d&msg=sTrnwa819MGdmGmkVzAhGw &user= &pw=>. In this example, though, there is a very simple solution which is, in fact, suggested by a similar circumstance in using print sources. This involves use of the abbreviation s.v. (for the Latin *sub verbo*, "under the word") in making citations to standard reference works such as encyclopedias and dictionaries which are organized into individual entries usually presented in alphabetical order. Doing so in this case would result in a citation referring to the location of the main URL of the website which included the search function. This would then indicate to the reader that the message containing the citation guide could be found by entering the word "citation" in that search utility:

```
<www.h-net.msu.edu>, s.v. "citation".
```

Both the *Chicago Manual* and Turabian's manual suggest that such citations using "s.v." should only be used in notes and not in bibliographies. However, we believe that in the case of electronic sources—although perhaps not for printed encyclopedias and dictionaries—using such a citation format even in bibliographies offers writers an appropriate solution to one of the difficulties posed in documenting modern electronic sources.

One word of caution: We do *not* recommend that you make such citations to materials you find using one of the Internet-wide search engines such as Yahoo, Google, or Alta Vista. Those search engines take you to individual web sites which you should document separately. To make your citation to the search engine would be as if you made a citation for a book by merely referring to library catalog in which you had first found a reference to it! Only use the s.v. format for electronic searches you make from the home page of a particular web site which contains within it the material you have used in your essay.

No doubt there will be other issues that arise in the next few years as historians and others scholars deal even more with evolving electronic technologies. We believe firmly that solutions to any documentation problems for source materials on the Internet and in other electronic formats are possible. It is not necessary and in fact inappropriate simply to avoid such sources for lack of previously standard conventions for making citations to them. Should you confront such problems, ask questions of your instructor or a reference librarian about how you might deal with them. And you may also use some of the following samples as a guide in making decisions about how to document your use of those, as well as other, sources you have used.

NOTES AND BIBLIOGRAPHIES

Here are some sample citations using the *Chicago Manual*/Turabian style. In this section we present only a few of the many types of sources and the variations on issues of authorship, title, location, and date. You may look to those two manuals, and the electronic citation guides we have mentioned, for further examples.

Notes

Endnotes are in the same style as footnotes; the only difference is that endnotes go at the end of the paper, before the bibliography. The following samples are listed by the type of source you document in your notes. Of course, each note should be preceded by the number which refers to the place in your essay where you want to document sources for what you have written.

A book with one author

Caroline Walker Bynum, *The Resurrection of the Body in Western Christianity, 200-1336* (New York: Columbia University Press, 1995), 13.

A book with more than one author

Stanley L. Engerman and Robert William Fogel, *Time on the Cross: The Economics of American Negro Slavery* (New York: Norton, 1989), 206.

A book in a series

Larry William Moses and Stephen A. Halkovic, Jr., *Introduction to Mongolian History and Culture*, Indiana University Uralic and Altaic Series, vol. 149 (Bloomington: Research Institute for Inner Asian Studies, Indiana University, 1985), 199.

A book that has been edited and/or translated

Martin Luther, *Lectures on Romans*, ed. and trans. Wilhelm Pauck (Philadelphia: The Westminster Press, 1961), 100.

An article in a book that is a collection of essays

Gabrielle Spiegel, "History and Postmodernism," in *The Postmodern History Reader*, ed. Keith Jenkins (London and New York: Routledge, 1997), 261.

Periodicals are, as the name indicates, published at regular intervals, and under that heading we include scholarly journals, popular magazines, and newspapers.

A scholarly journal article

> Denise S. Spooner, "A New Perspective on the Dream: Midwestern Images of Southern California in the Post-World War II Decades," *California History* 76, no. 1 (Spring 1997): 48.

The journal *California History* paginates every issue separately. Many journals, such as the *American Historical Review,* paginate consecutively throughout the year so that the first issue begins with page 1 and the last issue may end with page 1250, or whatever. In that case, omit the issue number.

Many publishers in these days of skyrocketing costs omit both volume number and issue number and leave only the date, which is almost always sufficient to locate the reference. Issues of popular magazines such as *Time, Newsweek,* and *Smithsonian* are always identified by the date alone.

An article in a popular magazine, paginated by issue

> Janet Waliach, "Daughter of the Desert," *Smithsonian,* April 1998, 125.

Newspapers are often published in sections. In the following note, the "A1" refers to section A, page one.

A newspaper article

> David E. Sanger, "Clinton Warns Japan: Fire Up Economy to Stem a Decline," *New York Times,* April 4,1998, A1.

A note that refers to a book review, whether published in a scholarly journal, a popular magazine, or a newspaper should begin with the name of the reviewer, followed by the title of the book reviewed and the name of its author(s), and then the details of where the review appears.

A book review

> Harvey Hames, review of *Rituals of Childhood: Jewish Acculturation in Medieval Europe,* by Ivan Marcus, *Journal of Jewish Studies* 48(Autumn 1997): 387.

For well known reference works, publication details are not usually included in notes.

An article in a reference source

> *Dictionary of the History of Ideas,* s.v. "Historiography," by Herbert Butterfield.

Information from a web site

> Joseph C. Miller, "History and Africa/Africa and History," <http://www.ecu.edu/african/sersas/jmahapa.htm>, 8 January 1999 [accessed 21 April 2001].

Notice that for web sites no page numbers are given, as they are usually not available.

A listserv message

> Richard Lobban, <RLobban@grog.ric.edu>, "REPLY: African Muslim Slaves in America," in H-Africa, <h-africa@msu.edu>, 4 August 1995, archived at <http://h-net.msu.edu/~africa/archives/august95>.

Many listserv messages are available in some form of electronic archive. If it is at all possible, the preference for historians would be to document that availability as a first choice in a citation. Precisely because so many listserv and e-mail messages are not available to most researchers in an electronic archive, some historians eschew them as sources. Yet just as historians may occasionally wish to document information received in private letters they have received, you may need to document a private e-mail message.

A private e-mail message

```
    Carol Jones <carol.jones@perseusbooks.com>,
private e-mail message to Melvin Page <pagem@
etsu.edu>, "The Chiwaya War," 23 April 2001.
```

A CD-ROM

```
    Oxford English Dictionary, 2d ed, [CD-ROM],
s.v. "warfare".
```

Notice in this case the period is put outside the quotation marks since is was not a part of the search, but is rather a part of the punctuation of the note.

An archival document

```
    Benjamin Bowman, manuscript letter to Joseph
Bowman, 24 July 1860, Bowman Family Collection,
acc. no. 23, Archives of Appalachia, East Tennessee
State University, Johnson City, Tenn.
```

Here are some samples of subsequent references used in note format for a few of the notes we have illustrated above.

Subsequent references

```
    Bynum, p. 14.
    Moses and Halkovic, p. 200.
    Luther, Lectures on Romans, p. 101.
```

Notice this example: It supposes there is more than one work by Luther used in the essay.

```
    Spooner, 49.
    Miller.
```

Notice that in this case no page numbers are used, as there are none available for this citation to a website.

```
    Bowman to Bowman, 24 Jul 1860.
```

Notice the use of a date to distinguish from other potential letters; the month is abbreviated as well.

Bibliographies

Bibliographies are placed at the end of a book or an essay to allow readers to see quickly what works have been cited in the body of the text. A bibliography shows whether the writer has consulted a wide variety of sources and whether he or she knows the latest literature in a field of inquiry.

Bibliographies comprise much the same information as notes, but bibliographies are alphabetized by the last name of the author, and the punctuation is somewhat different. In *Chicago Manual/ Turabian* style, the bibliographic entry does not use parentheses, and each entry is set apart using a "hanging indent" system easily created with a word-processing program. Here is the bibliographic entry of the book by Caroline Walker Bynum listed in a footnote above:

Book by a single author

Bynum, Caroline Walker. *The Resurrection of the Body in Western Christianity, 200-1336.* New York: Columbia University Press, 1995.

Notice the positions of the periods, the absence of parentheses, and the absence of page numbers. Bibliographic references to periodicals follow the same principles as those of books except that the first and last page numbers of articles are included.

An article in a periodical

Spooner, Denise S. "A New Perspective on the Dream: Midwestern Images of Southern California in the Post-World War II Decades." *California History* 76, no. 1 (Spring 1997): 45-57.

A bibliographical entry with multiple authors

Moses, Larry William, and Stephen A. Halkovic, Jr., *Introduction to Mongolian History and Culture.* Indiana University Uralic and Altaic Series, vol. 149. Bloomington: Research Institute for Inner Asian Studies, Indiana University, 1985.

A collection of essays by several authors

Hart, Albert Bushnell, ed. *Commonwealth History of Massachusetts.* Five volumes. New York: The States History Company, 1927, 1928.

A single article in a collection of essays

Spiegel, Gabrielle. "History and Postmodernism." In *The Postmodern History Reader,* edited by Keith Jenkins, 260-273. London and New York: Routledge, 1997.

A web site

Joseph C. Miller. "History and Africa/Africa and History." <http://www.ecu.edu/african/sersas/jmahapa.htm>. 8 January 1999 [accessed 21 April 2001].

A web site search

Encyclopedia Britannica. <www.britannica.com>. s.v. "Luther, Martin". [accessed 21 April 2001].

A CD-ROM

Oxford English Dictionary, 2d ed. [CD-ROM]. Oxford: Oxford University Press, 1992.

An archival collection

Bowman Family Collection. Accession no. 23. Archives of Appalachian, East Tennessee State University, Johnson City, Tenn.

As the few examples we have given may suggest to you, the moment you begin to do research and write about it, the more complex footnoting and bibliographies become. Turabian's manual is larger than this book, and as mentioned above, it is only an abridgment of the much larger *Chicago Manual of Style.* The good news is that common sense and care for precision and consistency can solve a multitude of problems and allow you to guide readers faithfully through the sources you have used, no matter what those sources may be.

Appendix A

■ ■ ■

Sample Student Research Paper

On the following pages you will find a sample research paper written for a course in world history using the process outlined in Chapter 4. Study the paper. Then study the questions about the paper at the end. Ask these same questions about any paper you write for a history course.

Pay close attention to the format of the paper. Note the title page, the footnotes, and the bibliography. The title page includes the title of the paper, the name of the author, the date the paper is turned in, the name of the course, the time of the class, and the name of the professor. The margins should be set at no less than one inch on all four sides of the page. ALWAYS number pages, but remember that the title page is not numbered, although it is considered page one of your paper.

Manifest Destiny: A Characteristic of Nations

BY PENNY M. SONNENBURG
East Tennessee State University
20 March 2001
History 4957: Colonialism and Imperialism
Professor Melvin Page
M 2:00—4:50 pm

More than a century before John L. O'Sullivan wrote the words reflective of the expansionist fervor that gripped the United States, of "our manifest destiny to overspread the continent,"[1] the essence of the idea was already a part of what would become our national heritage. Yet as late as the 1920s, Julius Pratt proclaimed confidently in the *American Historical Review* that O'Sullivan invented the phrase.[2] Now, over a century and a half after O'Sullivan penned those well known words, it should be apparent that the United States was not alone in its fervor and that O'Sullivan merely gave dramatic voice to what was a well developed national disposition with deep roots in the Western European tradition.

In *The Power of Ideals in American History,* Ephraim Adams construed the concept of "manifest destiny" as an inherent aspect of all countries. Adams elaborated that the "sense of destiny is an attribute of all nations and all peoples." He claimed that distinct emotions of various tribes and races provided an early understanding of "manifest destiny." Probably we would find that these tribes and races also felt themselves a "chosen people" set apart for some high purpose.[3]

Adams also implied that any great nation had a belief in its destiny—larger nations wanting a place in the sun while smaller, contented nations

[1] John L. O'Sullivan, "Annexation," *Democratic Review*, 17 (July and August 1845), in *Manifest Destiny and the Imperialism Question*, ed. Charles L. Sanford (New York: John Wiley & Sons, 1974), 28.

[2] Julius W. Pratt, "The Origin of 'Manifest Destiny'," *American Historical Review*, 32 (1927), 798.

[3] Ephraim Douglas Adams, *The Power of Ideals in American History*, (New York: AMS Press, Inc. 1969), 67.

were constantly on alert to avoid absorption by their more powerful neighbors. As historians, we can analyze and thereby illustrate that the concept of manifest destiny occurred long before 1845 and was not limited to the American people. The United States, beginning with its colonial past, utilized the essence of the concept, placing it on a higher philosophical plane. The nationalistic expansionist movement in the United States was based upon a moral ideology and appeared as an inherent quality justifying itself as a natural right.[4]

"Natural right" formed the historical foundation that was later used as an explanation and underlying ideology surrounding the manifest destiny movement. "Natural right" was basically defined as any right that "Nature," recognized in a "divinely supported system of 'natural law' inclusive of moral truths, bestows prior to or independently of political society." The beginnings of this idea can be traced back to Greek philosophers who wrote of "things that are right by nature, that is, inherently, and can be recognized by every rational being to be so."[5] Later stoic philosophers, and indeed basic Roman legal beliefs, followed the same reasoning that natural rights were among the truths contained in natural law. Sir Ernest Barker, in *Traditions of Civility,* addressed the natural law idea as a movement among the stoic thinkers of the Hellenistic age. The large and somewhat general expression "became a tradition of human civility which runs continuously from the Stoic teachers of the Porch to the American Revolution of 1776 and the French Revolution of

---

[4] Albert K. Weinberg, *Manifest Destiny: A Study of Nationalist Expansionism in American History* (New York: Johns Hopkins Press, 1958), 12.

[5] Weinberg, *Manifest Destiny*, 13-14.

1789."[6] For many centuries this was directly
considered part and parcel of church theology,
later adopted by the Catholic Church forming a core
element of church doctrine for teachers and early
canonists. This logic formed a rational basis for
the physical and moral universe, hence the "theory
of Natural Law had become in the sixteenth century,
and continued to remain during the seventeenth and
the eighteenth, an independent and rationalist
system professed and expounded by the philosophers
of the secular school of natural law."[7] Later
Christianity "harmonized these ideas of paganism
with its own theology by regarding natural law as
the expression of the eternal reason of God." And
thus natural right came to embrace two principles
in the western tradition—secular and sacred—and set
the stage for the "momentous pretension later to be
called nationalism." This powerful affirmation
enhanced an emerging idea that nationalities were
the most likely agencies for promotion of not only
the rights of particular groups, but also the
rights of mankind as a whole.[8] This tendency toward
an assertion of group entitlement confirmed for
Adams his view of early tribes and races employing
concepts of higher purpose, foreshadowing early
nationalistic leanings.

Based on this a priori condition, there is firm
ground for asserting the close relationships
between the ideas usually described as nationalism,
expansionism, ethnicity, natural law, and manifest
destiny. The rhetoric of politics, religion, and

---

[6] Sir Ernest Barker, *Traditions of Civility*
(Cambridge: Cambridge University Press, 1948), 312,
quoted by Gerard Watson, "The Natural Law and
Stoicism," in *Problems in Stoicism*, ed. A.A. Long
(London: The Atholone Press, 1971), 216.

[7] Barker, *Traditions of Civility*, 216.

[8] Weinberg, *Manifest Destiny*, 13-14.

philosophy throughout early European history
established a touchstone for these relationships.
And early historians of Europe were instrumental in
drawing attention to the connections. Tacitus,
Roman historian of the Germanic peoples, described
in his *Germania* such characteristics among the
people about whom he wrote. "In the peoples of
Germany," he declared, "there has been given to the
world a race untainted by intermarriage with other
races, a peculiar people and pure, like no one but
themselves."[9] Such tendencies were passed on to the
early populations of Great Britain who were
descendants of Germanic tribes. William Camden
confirms this when he wrote, in his *Remaines
concerning Britaine,* that "he saw God's hand in the
guiding of the Angles and Saxons to England."[10]
This version of the "chosen people" doctrine became
an early cornerstone of popular ideology in England
as the New Anglican church under Elizabeth adopted
the essence of its message.

Archbishop Matthew Parker, a major defender of
Anglo-Saxon literature and scholarship, along with
his secretary, John Joscelyn, began an inquiry of
pre-Norman English history. The purpose of their
study was an effort not only to prove the
ancientness of new English church customs but also
to promote an interest in general English history
during the Anglo-Saxon period. Archbishop Parker's
contemporary John Foxe particularly emphasized in
his 1563 *Acts and Monuments* the "uniqueness of the
English and their nature as 'a chosen people,'" with
a church lineage stretching back to Joseph of
Arimathea and his supposed visit to England, and
with John Wyclif as the true originator of the

---

[9] Quoted in Reginald Horsman, *Race and Manifest
Destiny*, (Cambridge: Harvard University Press,
1981), 12.

[10] Horsman, *Race and Manifest Destiny*, 12.

Reformation."[11] Following the English Revolution,
and especially after the Restoration of the
monarchy, "the idea of the English nation as the
crusading agent of God's will faded" into a minor
theme in English thought. But the historical roots
of the philosophy ran deep and were planted
especially on the frontiers of English
expansionism. It is no wonder then, that "Americans
never lost the belief that they were a special,
chosen people, a people destined to change the
world for the better."[12]

The ascendancy of the English view of the
Anglo-Saxons appeared as an inherent characteristic
in the American colonies. The post-Reformation
continental writers reinforced the myth produced by
two centuries of political and religious conflict.
"As colonial Englishmen the settlers in America
fully absorbed the mythical view of the English
past developed between 1530 and 1730."[13] Colonial
settlers did not limit their absorption to one
viewpoint. They also embraced and were inspired by
an emerging philosophy of nationalism. In an effort
to systematize nationalism, eighteenth-century
European philosophers provided the spark for
revolutionary movements of the period. The
diversity of thought found in the "culturally
nationalistic Herder, the democratic Rousseau, the
Tory Bolingbroke, and the liberal physiocrats" was
transplanted into the natural rights domain of the
American colonial psyche. These philosophers'
proto-nationalist doctrines basically included
one—and usually both—of two basic foundations of
natural right ideas. The first principle addressed
the "natural rights of groups to determine upon and
organize the desired form of government." The
second principle declared that nations were the

---

[11] Horsman, *Race and Manifest Destiny*, 10.

[12] Horsman, *Race and Manifest Destiny*, 82.

[13] Horsman, *Race and Manifest Destiny*, 15.

"natural agencies" for advancing not only the rights of particular groups but also the rights of all mankind.[14] One does not have to have an overactive imagination to recognize this characteristic in colonial America.

In *Manifest Destiny and Mission in American History, a Reinterpretation*, historian Frederick Merk links nationalism with expansionism. He asserts that expansionism was usually associated with ideology. Merk's validation of this point leads one past the early writings of natural right into an ideological framework for expansionism. His broad, global sweeps through expansionist ideology are summarized as he concludes of the causes: "In the case of Arab expansionism it was Islam; in Spanish expansionism, Catholicism; in Napoleonic expansionism, revolutionary liberalism; in Russian and Chinese expansionism, Marxian communism." In the United States an equivalent of these ideologies appeared as manifest destiny, and the main ingredients consisted of republicanism, democracy, freedom of religion, and Anglo-Saxonism.[15] The intellectual ship that carried the settlers across the wide Atlantic also altered, and then adopted, the "idea of natural right as the moral rationale of America's expansionism." In the early developmental period, the newly arrived Americans tended to stress the rights rather than the duties of natural law. "The conception of natural right was first used by New England clergymen in behalf of right of ecclesiastical independency." In 1760 the concept escaped from the pulpits into the public discussion arena as Americans became concerned with their own political rights under English rule. This ideological transformation reached an initial

---

[14] Weinberg, *Manifest Destiny*, 13-14.

[15] Frederick Merk, *Manifest Destiny and Mission in American History, A Reinterpretation* (New York: Alfred A. Knopf, 1963), vii-ix.

climax with inclusion of the "inalienable natural rights with which their Creator had endowed them [Americans]" in the Declaration of Independence confirming the United States' belief in its "chosenness." Americans assumed the position "among the powers of the earth, the separate and equal station to which the Laws of Nature and Nature's God entitle them." Assuming the position of natural rights guardian, Americans justified the "right of revolution when governments became destructive of natural rights."[16]

The end of the American Revolution empowered the new nation and set it along a course that engaged the country in the manifest destiny phenomenon. This total embrace of a powerful movement allowed the misnomer that manifest destiny was a uniquely American feature. Early American history is laced with examples of the doctrine that have been used throughout as situational justification of the means to the end. In 1801 Jefferson's application of diplomatic and military pressure induced Napoleon to negotiate with the United States for sale of New Orleans and a slice of coastal territory to the east. Much to Jefferson's surprise, in 1803 Napoleon sold all of the immense Louisiana territory to the United States. This enabled Jefferson to realize his main objective: possession of New Orleans and ultimate control of the mouth of the Mississippi, thus providing the much-needed outlet to world markets for the interior of the new nation.[17] Acquisition of the Louisiana Purchase also perpetuated the expansionist movement of the United States.

This expansionism continued as a nationally heartfelt but nameless movement. As early as 1818

---

[16] Weinberg, *Manifest Destiny*, 16.

[17] David Goldfield, et al., *The American Journey, A History of the United States*, (Upper Saddle River, New Jersey: Prentice Hall, 1998), 261.

Andrew Jackson applied his own understanding of President Monroe's instructions and led military forces into Spanish-held Florida, destroying the Indians in his path; he set into motion the natural rights claim of Americans to possession of any land that they wanted.[18] Further use of the still unnamed principle appeared as an American assumption that its destiny was that of a world power. In 1822 the Monroe Doctrine—warning the whole of Europe to stay out of the Western Hemisphere—illustrated James Monroe's belief in this idea. Monroe was certainly not alone in this belief, although there was a small vocal opposition which made the yet unnamed doctrine a disputed philosophy.

The opposition movement exposed a different side to Americans as being the "chosen people." In an 1837 letter to Henry Clay, William E. Channing wrote that "we are a restless people, prone to encroachment, impatient of the ordinary laws of progress." Channing feared the strength that the country felt at extending its boundaries—by natural right—from shore to shore was fraught with dire consequences. "We boast of our rapid growth," he continued in his letter to Clay, "forgetting that, throughout nature, noble growths are slow. . . . Already endangered by our greatness, we cannot advance without imminent peril to our institutions, union, prosperity, virtue, and peace."[19] Opposition, however, seems to have emboldened the proponents of the doctrine which was only then surfacing in open expression.

What seemed to be the opinion of a majority of the American people at the time was featured not

---

[18] Goldfield, et al., *The American Journey*, 277.

[19] Quoted in Michael T. Lubragge, "Manifest Destiny," in *The American Revolution—an .HTML project*, <http://odur.let.rug.nl/~usa/E/manifest>, 17 April 2001.

only in John O'Sullivan's 1845 editorial in the *Democratic Review* but also in another article published in the same journal that year. This also addressed the Texas annexation issue and justified the addition of the new state. "Texas has been absorbed into the Union in the inevitable fulfillment of the general law which is rolling our population westward." The author contended that Texas "was disintegrated from Mexico in the natural course of events, by a process perfectly legitimate on its Union was not only inevitable, but the most natural, right and proper thing in the world."[20] It is not ironic that the article appeared in this particular *Review*, as it was the same journal that finally gave a name—hence a formal justification—for what was the right of Americans: our Manifest Destiny.

Precursors to American predominance had been played out, and history was set to be made, all in the name of Manifest Destiny. This is a classic example of how, when doctrines gain names, they in turn gain legitimacy and ultimately power. The combination of the idealistic vision of social perfection through God and the pride of American nationalism in the mid-nineteenth century filled an American ideological need for domination of the hemisphere from pole to pole, as Monroe had implied. This was ultimately based on the concept of Americans' possessing a divine providence. The strong belief of God's will for American expansion over the whole of the continent and to ultimately control the country led to a guiding call to human destiny. "It was white man's burden to conquer and christianize the land," as Kipling envisioned at the end of nineteenth century. This expanded the Puritan notion of a "city on a hill" and was secularized into Manifest Destiny, albeit a materialistic, religious, and utopian destiny.[21]

---

[20] Quoted in Lubragge, "Manifest Destiny."

[21] Lubragge, "Manifest Destiny."

This eventually led to the fear that foreigners crossing the national frontier borders might hamper the security of the United States. The most reasonable answer was to conquer land beyond those borders and expand to other areas. This became evident when Albert T. Beveridge arose in the United States Senate and espoused the view—with utmost certainty—that "Anglo-Saxon [America] was destined to rule the world" and went on to state that "He [God] has made us the master organizers of the world to establish system where chaos reigns."[22] In speaking so boldly, Beveridge introduced an international dimension to American Manifest Destiny that justified the 1867 purchase of Alaska from Russia for $7,200,000. The price of being a world empire had risen from its earlier purchase of Louisiana from Napoleon! Indeed, not only the price, but the arrogance of this doctrine was on the rise as the expansionist fervor grew following the Spanish-American War. Congress went so far as to call for annexation of all Spanish territories. Newspapers of the time were more extreme in suggesting the annexation of Spain itself.

Aspirations of an American empire were echoed in the views of other expansionists, including Theodore Roosevelt, former President Harrison, and Captain Alfred T. Mahan. Indeed the latter's treatise on the importance of naval power in international affairs was especially influential. Such voices fed what seemed to be an insatiable desire once again, manifesting itself in 1898 when America decided that it wanted control of Hawaii and took it—oddly not quite so differently as when Andrew Jackson took Florida nearly a century before. The supposed American mission to the islands came to fruition in 1959 when the United States made Hawaii its fiftieth state.[23]

---

[22] Quoted in Lubragge, "Manifest Destiny."

[23] Lubragge, "Manifest Destiny."

Throughout American history the dual visions of the American people—of a divine providence destined by God to direct national expansion, or of a natural right to extend liberty (our own version, of course) to other parts of the world—seemed to complement each other. Once again, it appeared that the means ultimately justified the end. As a people we embraced an unnamed, but not unknown, doctrine and made it our own. And, as in our previous history, we have taken concepts, ideologies, and policies—altering them to fit our own needs—and then applying them to our own country.

While this process is not totally detrimental, it hinders our ability to understand and examine American history as a part of the world, as well as our own national, history. When faced with attempting to understand the philosophy of destiny and the concept of being a "chosen people," it is most beneficial to widen our lens and focus on a broader picture. When this occurs, we can then understand that the United States did not create a new doctrine but simply embellished upon principles that can be traced back to earlier "chosen people" and their own individual views of natural right and nationalism. This philosophy began as far back—if not farther—as the Greek philosophy of Stoicism. Viewed that way, manifest destiny is a necessary requirement for all societies seeking a higher purpose for their own nation and people. This is not totally inconceivable, since "all nations that are worth anything, always have had, and always will have, some ideal of national destiny, and without it, would soon disappear, and would deserve their fate."[24]

---

[24] Adams, *Power of Ideals*, 68.

Bibliography

Adams, Ephraim Douglass. *The Power of Ideals in American History*. New York: AMS Press, Inc. 1969.

Haynes, Sam W. "Manifest Destiny." Arlington: University of Texas Press. <http://www.pbs.org/kera/usmexicanwar/dialogues/prelude/manifest/d2heng.html>. [Accessed 2 Feb 2001].

Horsman, Reginald. *Race and Manifest Destiny.* Cambridge: Harvard University Press. 1981.

LaFeber, Walter. "The World and the United States." *American Historical Review*. 100(October 1995): 1015-1033.

Long, A.A., ed. *Problems in Stoicism*. London: The Atholone Press. 1971.

Lubragge, Michael T. "Manifest Destiny." *The American Revolution—an .HTML project.* <http:// odur.let.rug.nl/~usa/E/manifest>, 17 April 2001.

Merk, Frederick. *Manifest Destiny and Mission in American History, A Reinterpretation.* New York: Alfred A. Knopf. 1963.

O'Sullivan, "Annexation," *Democratic Review*, 17 (July and August 1845), in *Manifest Destiny and the Imperialism Question*, ed. Charles L. Sanford (New York: John Wiley & Sons, 1974), 26-34.

Pratt, Julius W. "The Origin of 'Manifest Destiny'" *American Historical Review*, 32(1927), 798.

Sanford, Charles L., ed. *Manifest Destiny and the Imperialism Question*. New York: John Wiley & Sons, Inc. 1974.

Webb, Walter Prescott. "The Frontier and the 400 Year Boom." In *The Turner Thesis concerning the Role of the Frontier in American History*, ed. George Rogers Clark, 87-95. Boston: D.C. Heath and Company. 1956.

Weinberg, Albert K. *Manifest Destiny: A Study of Nationalist Expansionism in American History*. New York: Johns Hopkins Press. 1958.

THINGS TO NOTICE ABOUT THIS PAPER

This paper is more a historiographic essay than some traditional history papers. Nonetheless, it still presents primary sources, secondary sources, and the interpretations of the author to arrive at a thesis: that "Manifest Destiny" was not merely a phenomenon of American history. The paper is more than a mere collection of sources pasted together. The writer has thought about the material and has arrived at some interpretations that help explain it. She has inferred much from her sources and has treated some of the writings of philosophers and historians as primary sources, as she should.

The author's own point of view is unmistakable: She points out a long-standing interpretation of American history—one which has sometimes captured the popular imagination—and indicates how her interpretation differs. She identifies the source of the phrase and then traces the roots of the essential idea back through English history to its ancient roots. She arrives at a judgment about the effect of this on the history of the United States, but she does not preach to the reader. A historian can make judgments on whether certain ideas or actions in the past were good or bad. Historians do that sort of thing all the time. But it is not acceptable in the field of history to rage about events in the past as if your readers must be persuaded more by your emotions than by your evidence and reasoning. Trust your readers. They do not read this paper to see how upset or self-righteous the writer is; they read to see how a fundamental idea about American history actually ties the United States into a broad reach of global history.

The paper is documented throughout so readers may look up the evidence should they want to know more about it. Notice particularly how Ms. Sonnenburg has used primary sources, identifying them even in the writings of others. This helps prevent the paper from being a collage of what other historians have written about manifest destiny. This technique is highly valuable, especially when you face limitations of direct access to the original primary sources.

The thoughtfulness of the author in dealing with her sources is enough to make us feel that we have learned something important from someone who has taken pains to become an authority on an important aspect of United States history and see how it has larger historical implications.

Answer the questions below by studying this sample paper. You would do well to ask these questions about your own writing:

Writer's Checklist

_____ ✔ What sentence or sentences near the beginning of the paper announce the writer's thesis, the main idea that controls the paper?

_____ ✔ How does the writer use quotations? Why does she use shorter quotations, rather than larger block quotations, throughout? Where does she seem to paraphrase instead?

_____ ✔ What form do footnotes take? Why does the form sometimes change?

_____ ✔ Where does the writer use secondary sources? Can you show where she disagrees with some of her secondary sources?

_____ ✔ Where does the author make inferences? That is, where does she make plausible suggestions about the meaning of various texts when the meaning is not explicit in the text itself?

_____ ✔ Which paragraphs in the essay are primarily narrative? Where does the author write in a more expository mode?

_____ ✔ Where are arguments in the essay?

_____ ✔ Where does the writer make her own judgments clear?

_____ ✔ Where does the author use simile and metaphor to good effect?

_____ ✔ In what ways does the conclusion of the paper mirror some of the ideas in the opening?

Appendix B

. . .

Book Reviews

Reviewing books is an essential part of the historian's profession. Book reviews represent an assessment of the writing of other historians. Writing book reviews is also a good way to train yourself in understanding how the discipline of history works. Such writing is often complicated and demanding. Reviewers do report on the content of the book, but they also evaluate the work by discussing matters such as the author's logic and organization, evidence and conclusions, and sometimes even the writer's style.

REVIEWING AS A SPECIAL FORM OF WRITING

While writing a book review does require many of the same writing skills we have discussed in this book, it is also a special form of historical writing. You are expected to engage with the historical ideas of another author, to report on and evaluate them, and to present your conclusions to other historians. Such an effort will draw you into debates about historical subjects. That is why many students are asked to write book reviews in their history classes. But keep in mind there are several types of book reviews.

Popular reviews are generally written for publications intended for an informed readership, such as *The Atlantic*, *Harper's*, *The New Republic*, *The New York Review*, or other widely circulated magazines. Some newspapers, such as *The New York Times* and the *Washington Post*, also carry similar reviews in some of their editions. Occasionally popular reviews range far and wide, extending beyond the contents of the book to issues it raises in the reviewer's mind. Thus, some popular reviews take the form of extended essays on particular subjects which might include the topic of the book or books under review, or even occasionally narrower aspects of that topic. While these are frequently very interesting essays, they do not always offer very practical models for the types of reviews you may be asked to write.

Two other types of book reviews are more important as guides to your own writing. The first, which we call *academic reviews*, usually appear in scholarly journals such as the *American Historical Review*, the *Journal of World History* or *The Historian*. These are frequently much shorter than popular reviews—often little more than five hundred words—and are generally intended for a professional, scholarly audience. On occasion, historical journals may also publish one or two longer "review essays" which more closely approximate what we have termed popular reviews. But for historians, these review essays frequently focus on the important scholarly issues raised by the book or books the reviewer is considering. We suggest that you look at the book reviews and review essays in historical journals and also at the H-Net Reviews Web site we mentioned in Chapter 4; these will give you some idea of the way historians generally prepare and present book reviews.

As an example of an academic review, intended for a professional audience of historians, here is a review written for the *Journal of American History* by historian Edward Countryman:

The Shoemaker and the Tea Party: Memory and the American Revolution. By Alfred F. Young. (Boston: Beacon, 1999. xx, 262 *pp.* $24.00, ISBN 0-8070-7140-4.)

"Gem-like" is one of the highest terms of praise in Alfred F. Young's vocabulary. I have heard him apply it only twice. Almost two decades ago he published a gem-like extended essay called "George Robert Twelves Hewes: A Boston Shoemaker and the Memory of the American Revolution" in the *William and Mary Quarterly*. The essay won that journal's annual best-article prize. Now, as part of an ongoing project about the intertwined themes of revolutionary Boston and historical memory, he has turned that essay into a book.

Part I of *The Shoemaker and the Tea Party* reprints the original essay, broken now into twelve short chapters and slightly amended in the light of Young's thinking since 1982. Part II considers how the shoemaker Hewes became a living subject of historical memory in his very old age and how the events in which he took part emerged as an iconic part of revolutionary historical imagery. Taking as his subject what ought to have been obvious (but, as so often happens, was not obvious at all), Young notes the more-than-coincidence of the emergence of the term "tea party" to describe the destruction of the East India Company's tea in December 1773 and the emergence of Hewes as one of the party's/destruction's hallowed veterans six decades later.

It seems unlikely that a revolution-era specialist is unaware of Young's original essay, but a summary remains appropriate. Influenced by the work of E. P. Thompson and Carlo Ginzburg, Young set out to explore the Revolution meaning in the life of one very ordinary man, who proved under close examination to be extraordinary. Hewes was a "nobody" all his life, until, in very old age, he had his Warholian moment of celebrity. He was born poor in Boston, lived poor there and in New York State, and died poor. There is no little irony in the fact that after the Revolution his loyalist brother Shubael, not he, acquired the honorific "gentleman" to put after his name. But in experiential terms Hewes was rich. He moved from shaking with fear at the very thought of being in John Hancock's house to facing down arrogant officers (British and American alike) and talking on equal terms with George Washington. If life brought Hewes disappointment in material terms, it taught him a great deal about equality.

Young's long-term project has been to recover a revolutionary American Revolution. But, like Thompson, he never has allowed perspective to turn into wishful thinking. He demonstrates that the destruction of the tea was an entirely revolutionary act and that Hewes lived a revolutionary life. He also shows how the late-life fame of Hewes served conservative political purposes. That need not have been so.

Other possibilities for historical memory existed, and the life of Hewes could have made good sense within the framework those possibilities provided.

"Definitive" is not in my professional vocabulary. But this elegant book does deserve the description "gem-like." The popular success it already enjoys suggests that a public that is hungry for history that is both good and accessible recognizes that point.[1]

You can recognize Professor Countryman's admiration in this review. But you also get a real sense that the reviewer has understood the purpose as well as the historiographic context of the book he is reviewing. What you may be asked to write in one or more of your courses should bear some similarities to this review; we refer to these class assignments as *scholastic reviews*. They are generally longer than most academic reviews and are intended for a more scholarly audience—your instructors and fellow students. They are much more like the "review essays" we mentioned above which sometimes appear in scholarly journals. Your instructor may provide very specific instructions about what should appear in such a review; if so, heed them. But here are some general guidelines that should help you in writing better book reviews no matter what your specific instructions may be.

1. **Read the book!** That may seem self-evident, but it remains perhaps the most important advice about writing a book review. Now and then even professional historians don't read the books they review in journals. You can see their errors when outraged authors write to protest; occasionally you will find such communications in historical journals. Don't let that happen to you! If you find and read one or more academic reviews of the book you have been assigned or have selected to review you may learn a great deal. But that is not

---

[1] Edward Countryman, review of *The Shoemaker and the Tea Party*, by Alfred E. Young, *Journal of American History* 87(2000): 648–649.

a substitute for reading the book and making your own judgments. Also remember: Fundamental honesty requires for you to say if you take something—ideas or quotations—for your book review from a review someone else has written.

2. **Identify the author, but don't waste time on needless or extravagant claims about her or him.** It is a cliché to say that the author is "well qualified" to write a book. You may write briefly about the author's background and perhaps the work he or she put into creating the book you are reviewing. But don't belabor the point.

3. **Always give the author's major theme or thesis, his or her motive for writing the book.** How do you find that theme or thesis? Read the book thoughtfully. Always read the introduction or the preface. Students in a hurry may skip the introduction, thinking they are saving time. That can be a serious mistake. Authors often use introductions to state the reasons that impelled them to write their books. Indeed, we recommend you read the preface, the introduction, and the last chapter of a book before you read the complete work. Few writers can bear to leave their books without a parting shot: they want to be sure readers get the point! Reviewers should take advantage of that impulse. Some of our students object to our advice that they read the last chapter first. We remind them that history books are not novels, and good history books—as well as shorter essays—almost never have surprise endings. By reading the last chapter, you see where the author is heading as you read the entire book. And always remember the terms "theme" and "thesis" are not quite the same as the subject. The subject of the book may be the biography of Winston Churchill, prime minister of Great Britain during World War II. The theme or thesis, however, may be that Churchill was a great wartime leader but a poor interpreter of the post-war world.

4. **Summarize, but only briefly, the evidence the author presents in support of the thesis.** Do not fall into the habit of

writing a summary of the book as if you were writing a report rather than a review. This approach seldom can be translated into a successful book *review*. Don't try to report every interesting detail in the book. Leave something for readers to discover on their own. But it frequently is a good idea to recount some interesting incidents. Tell a story or two from the book. You may also wish to consider the types of evidence the author has used and particularly the effort to rely upon primary sources.

5. **Consider quoting a line or two here and there to give the flavor of the text.** Quote selectively but fairly. The prose of the author you review may help spice up your own review. But avoid long chunks of quotation. You must show your readers that you have absorbed the book you review.

6. **Avoid lengthy comments about the style of the book.** Saying that the style is good, bad, interesting, or tedious is fine. If a book is especially well written or if it is incomprehensible, you may quote a sentence to illustrate a good or bad style, but don't belabor the point. Generalizations such as, "This book is interesting," or, "This book is boring," do little to enhance your review. If you do your job in the review, readers can tell whether you find it interesting or boring. And remember, if you are bored, the fault may be in you rather than the book. An Ancient History professor at the University of Tennessee, when one of us said reading Plutarch was boring, declared sternly, "Mr. Marius, you have no right to be bored with Plutarch." Both of us agree he was right.

7. **Don't feel compelled to say negative things about the book.** If you find inaccuracies, say so. If you disagree with the writer's interpretation here and there, say that, too, giving your reasons. However, you should avoid passionate attacks on the book. Scholarship is not always courteous, but it should be. Reviewers who launch savage attacks on books usually make fools of themselves. Remember, too, that petty complaints about the book may also make you look foolish or unfair. Don't waste time pointing out typos

unless they change the meaning the author intends. Always remember that every good book has flaws. The author may make some minor errors in fact or some questionable judgments. Even so, the book may be extremely valuable. Don't condemn a book outright because you find some mistakes. Try to judge the book as a whole.

8. **Judge the book the author has written.** You may wish the author had written a different book. You might write a different book yourself. But the author has written *this* book. If the book did not need to be written, if it adds nothing to our knowledge of the field, if it makes conclusions unwarranted by the evidence, say so. But don't review the book as if it should be another book.

9. **Try to bring something from your own experience— your reading, your thoughts, your reflections, your recollections—to the book.** If you are reviewing a book about early twentieth-century China, and if you have been fortunate enough to have traveled in China, you may bring your own impressions to the review of the book. Try to make use of a broad part of your education when you review a book. If you have read other books in other classes that are relevant to this class, say something about those books in your review. If you know facts the author has overlooked, say so. But avoid writing as if you possess independent knowledge of the author's subject when in fact you have taken all you know from the book itself. Don't pretend to be an expert when you are not. Be honest.

A SAMPLE STUDENT REVIEW

The following review, also of Alfred Young's *The Shoemaker and the Tea Party*, was written by a student. Consider how this review differs from that of Professor Countryman and also how it touches on many of the same points.

A Common Man and the American Revolution

A Review of Alfred F. Young, *The Shoemaker and the Tea Party: Memory and the American Revolution*

BY SABRINA SHILAD
East Tennessee State University
February 26, 2001
History 4037: The American Revolution
Professor Dale Schmitt

Alfred F. Young's 1999 book, *The Shoemaker and the Tea Party,* allows him to express his views on the American Revolution and the position that a common man would take during this time. The book is divided into two sections; the first part traces the life of George Robert Twelves Hewes, and the second half deals with the impact of the revolution concerning the town of Boston and how this relates to George Robert Twelves Hewes. The book gives a clear insight about what it would have been like to be a common mechanic in Boston during revolutionary times.

Alfred F. Young spent close to twenty years working on *The Shoemaker and the Tea Party*. Young became interested in the American Revolution when he was a graduate student at Columbia University. He obtained his doctorate at Northwestern University, where he specialized in American history. Young then taught in several different universities in Connecticut, New Jersey, and Illinois. Since 1990, he has been a senior research fellow at the Newberry Library. The predecessor to Young's book was an essay published in the *William and Mary Quarterly* in 1981. The success of the essay in the academic community spurred Young to give a second life to the essay and to make *The Tea Party and the Shoemaker* accessible to a broader audience.

The book begins by introducing the reader to George Robert Twelves Hewes. He is first presented

through the two major biographies written about him
in 1834 and 1835. Both of these books describe
him to be the last surviving participant in the
Boston Tea Party. These two biographies are
significant because they are the first recorded
instances in which the destruction of the tea was
called the Boston Tea Party. James Hawkes and
Benjamin Bussey Thatcher, the original two
biographers, "sifted" through the memories of the
old man, 93 at the time, to retrieve the
reminiscences and feelings from sixty to eighty
years earlier.

George Robert Twelves Hewes was born in 1742
to a poor tanner in Boston. He was the sixth of
nine children, but only three older brothers and
one younger brother survived childhood. Hewes was a
very active boy and frequently got into trouble.
The violent punishments he received as a child
formed in him a very kind mind that did not want to
see anyone harmed. Because there was no one to help
pay for his apprenticeship in a respectable
profession, Hewes was apprenticed to a shoemaker,
which was considered one of the lower mechanic jobs
that one could acquire.

Hewes was involved in three of the most
significant acts in late colonial and revolutionary
Boston: the massacre, tea party, and tarring and
feathering John Malcolm. In the massacre, Hewes was
an unarmed protester who caught James Caldwell
after James was injured. Hewes chose to observe the
events of the massacre without becoming a
participant. However, Hewes was actively involved
in the tea party and was one of the "semi-invited"
men who destroyed the British East India Company's
tea. He was given a slightly elevated rank on the
ships by the Sons of Liberty due to his ability to
whistle loudly. While on the ship, Hewes believed
that he helped to throw a chest of tea overboard
with John Hancock. Further, one might go so far as
to say that Hewes was partly responsible for the
tarring and feathering of John Malcolm. Malcolm

threatened to beat a small boy with a cane for running into him. Hewes stopped Malcolm and Hewes was then clobbered over the head by Malcolm. The mob then proceeded to strip Malcolm and tar and feather him. Ironically, when Hewes awoke from his forced slumber, he ran after the mob attempting to cover Malcolm's naked body with a blanket.

Hewes became well known for his long name and short stature. Only 5'1", he was too short to enlist in the military. However, Hewes later became involved in the militia, serving for a total of twenty months in a variety of capacities. During the time of his militia service he was married to Sally Sumner, a wash-woman, who produced for him sixteen children. As a militia seaman, Hewes was supposed to have opportunities to make money— through buccaneer activities—to help support his wife and family. However, he made very little money on these voyages because the captains cheated him and would not pay him or give him his share of the bounty. Hewes was a poor man for most of his life and had to be supported by his children in his elder years.

The second portion of the book focused on the entire town of Boston and how the public viewed each of the major events. Young emphasizes public remembrance of the revolution and how the memory was shaped in the public mind. The controlling bodies of the city forced much of Boston to forget the events of the revolution by only emphasizing particular events and forcing many holidays to go uncelebrated. Individual people and actions were erased from memories, and all that was remembered was that George Washington saved the nation.

Alfred Young's biography of George Robert Twelves Hewes is very well written and allows the reader to easily follow along. The writing style that Young uses made the book enjoyable to read and allowed the reader to stay focused on the subject. The reader actually became involved in Hewes's story, wondering what Hewes was going to do next. Young avoids verbose sentences and presents his points in a very simple manner.

Most readers know about the examples Young uses in the book. This prevented the reader from becoming overwhelmed with dates, events, and people. Commonly, historical writers assume that the reader has a well developed knowledge on the subject, leaving the average reader lost in an abyss of names. Young avoids this dilemma by simplifying his explanations of the revolutionary acts mentioned in his book.

Young, however, throughout the beginning of the book draws extensively from the other two biographies written about Hewes. The quotations from Thatcher and Hawkes's biographies on Hewes seemed excessively long and frequent. It becomes so excessive that the reader may consider reading the other biographies as opposed to spending time with Young's summation of the other books.

The most powerful aspect of the book is its explanation of how the lower-class citizen in Boston reacted to the "legendary" events surrounding the Revolution. This is significant because there is very little documentation about the concerns of simple people during the Revolution. The problems with money, illness, and having a successful business are all addressed in Young's book. The reader becomes aware how challenging it was to support a family on a meager income. Young also explains to the reader alternative ways of making money that were necessary to survive, such as fishing for the soldiers and working for the militia.

Alfred F. Young's book was very educational and helpful. The book could explain details of the revolution to the average person without causing mystification or confusion. *The Shoemaker and the Tea Party* was an outstanding biography and analysis of the events in Boston before the official beginning of the revolution as well as how the city

reacted after the revolution. Young's book clearly
shows what revolutionary life was like for the
common, poor man—the mechanics, as they were
called—and to what extent the common people would
have been involved in riotous demonstrations.

THINGS TO NOTICE
ABOUT THESE REVIEWS

In comparing the two reviews, consider how both focus on some details about the personal life of the subject of this biography and how
they recognize the efforts of the book's author to place his subject in
a larger historical context. Which of the reviews deals most with the
details of the person who is the subject of the book? And which is
more concerned about the historiographic place of the book itself in
the study of American history? Can you recognize some of the differences between an academic review and a scholastic review from
studying these two examples? As you make these comparisons,
think about these key questions which you might also use to examine the book reviews that you write.

Writer's Checklist

_____ ✔ Have these reviewers given evidence they have
read the book?

_____ ✔ Is the main theme or thesis of the book adequately
identified?

_____ ✔ Are both the evidence and the argument used to
support the central thesis of the book clear?

_____ ✔ Is the writing style of the book's author adequately considered? Would quotations from the
book help in giving the readers of the reviews a
better sense of the writing style?

_____ ✔ Are the judgments of the book both temperate and
sound? Is the book reviewed the book that was
written?

_____ ✔ Has either reviewer succeeded in bringing something personal to the review?

_____ ✔ Do the reviewers assess the significance of the
book?

CREDITS

■ ■ ■

221

INDEX

■ ■ ■

For our children—
Richard, Fred, and John
Megan, Melanie, and Michael
And our adventures together exploring history,
at home and around the world.

Senior Vice President/Publisher: Joseph Opiela
Acquisitions Editor: Susan Kunchandy
Executive Marketing Manager: Carlisle Paulson
Senior Production Manager: Eric Jorgensen
Project Coordination, Text Design, and Electronic Page Makeup:
    UG / GGS Information Services, Inc.
Cover Design Manager: John Callahan
Cover Art: Collage by Michael Staats using the following images: [Chief Joseph,
    Montana Historical Society; Mark Twain © Bettman/Corbis; Queen Liliuokalani
    © Corbis; Telegraph © Bettman/Corbis; Steamboats © Hulton Getty/Liaison
    Agency; Abraham Lincoln, Library of Congress; Ulysses S. Grant, Library of
    Congress.]
Manufacturing Buyer: Roy Pickering
Printer and Binder: R. R. Donnelley & Sons, Inc.
Cover Printer: Coral Graphic Services

Library of Congress Cataloging-in-Publication Data

Marius, Richard.
    A short guide to writing about history.—4th ed. / Richard Marius, Melvin E. Page.
        p. cm.—(The short guide series)
    Includes bibliographical references and index.
    ISBN 0-321-09300-3 (alk. paper)
    1. Historiography. 2. History—Methodology. 3. History—Research. 4. Academic
writing. I. Page, Melvin E. (Melvin Eugene), 1944- II. Title.

D13.M294 2001
907'.2—dc21

                                                        2001050233

Please visit our website at *http://www.ablongman.com*

ISBN 0-321-09300-3

1 2 3 4 5 6 7 8 9 10—DOC—04 03 02 01

TO WRITING
ABOUT HISTORY

. . .

Fourth Edition

RICHARD MARIUS
Harvard University

MELVIN E. PAGE
East Tennessee State University

Longman

New York   Boston   San Francisco
London   Toronto   Sydney   Tokyo   Singapore   Madrid
Mexico City   Munich   Paris   Cape Town   Hong Kong   Montreal